AN INTRODUCTION TO DISTRIBUTED AND PARALLEL PROCESSING

COMPUTER SCIENCE TEXTS

CONSULTING EDITORS

K. J. BOWCOCK
BSc, FBCS, FIMA
Department of Computer Science,
University of Aston in Birmingham

C. M. REEVES
MA, PhD, FIMA
Professor of Computer Science,
University of Keele

K. WOLFENDEN
MA
Emeritus Professor of Information Processing,
University College, London

COMPUTER SCIENCE TEXTS

An Introduction to Distributed and Parallel Processing

JOHN A. SHARP
Lecturer in Computer Science
University College of Swansea

BLACKWELL SCIENTIFIC PUBLICATIONS

OXFORD LONDON EDINBURGH

BOSTON PALO ALTO MELBOURNE

TO MY PARENTS

© 1987 by
Blackwell Scientific Publications
Editorial offices:
Osney Mead, Oxford, OX2 0EL
  (*Orders:* Tel. 0865 240201)
8 John Street, London, WC1N 2ES.
23 Ainslie Place, Edinburgh, EH3 6AJ.
52 Beacon Street, Boston
  Massachusetts 02108, USA.
667 Lytton Avenue, Palo Alto
  California 94301, USA.
107 Barry Street, Carlton
  Victoria 3053, Australia.

All rights reserved. No part of this
publication may be reproduced, stored in
a retrieval system, or transmitted, in any
form or by any means, electronic
mechanical, photocopying, recording or
otherwise, without the prior permission of
the copyright owner.

First published 1987

Phototypeset by
Oxford Computer Typesetting

**Printed and bound in Great Britain
by Billing & Sons Limited, Worcester.**

DISTRIBUTORS

USA and Canada
Blackwell Scientific Publications Inc
P O Box 50009, Palo Alto
California 94303.
  (*Orders:* Tel. (415) 965-4081)

Australia
Blackwell Scientific Publications
  (Australia) Pty Ltd
107 Barry Street
Carlton, Victoria 3053.
  (*Orders:* Tel. (03) 347 0300)

British Library
Cataloguing in Publication Data

Sharp, J.A. (John Anthony), 1955–
  An introduction to distributed and parallel
  processing. — (Computer science texts)
  1. Parallel processing (Electronic computers)
  2. Electronic data processing — Distributed
  processing
  I. Title II. Series
  004'.35 QA76.6

ISBN 0-632-01745-7
ISBN 0-632-01462-8 Pbk

Library of Congress
Cataloging in Publication Data

Sharp, J.A. (John A.), 1955–
  An introduction to distributed and parallel
  processing.
  (Computer science texts)
  Bibliography: p.
  Includes index.
  1. Electronic data processing — Distributed
  processing.
  2. Parallel processing (Electronic computers)
  I. Title II. Series
  QA76.9.D5S52 004'.35 86-32735

ISBN 0-632-01745-7
ISBN 0-632-01462-8 (Pbk.)

Contents

    Preface, vii
1   Introduction, 1

Part 1: Parallel Computers, 9

2   Parallelism and Interaction, 11
3   A Brief History of Parallelism, 23
4   Parallel Architectures, 32

Part 2: Distributed Systems, 53

5   Fully Distributed Processing Systems, 55
6   Networks and Interconnection Structures, 63
7   Designing a Distributed Processing System, 78

Part 3: Programming for Distributed and Parallel Processing, 89

8   Compiling Programs for Parallel Execution, 91
9   Programming for Array Processors, 106
10 Programming with Shared Memory, 113
11 Communicating Sequential Processes and Occam, 124

Part 4: Future Computer Architectures, 139

12 Data Flow Computing, 141
13 The Functional Approach, 150
14 The Connection Machine, 160

15 Summary and Conclusions, 166

    Cumulative Bibliography, 169
    Index, 171

Preface

This book is based on a series of notes prepared for a one term course given at the University College of Swansea. The course was aimed at a class of mainly final year undergraduates.

After an introductory chapter the text is organized into four main parts. The first part introduces the concept of parallelism (Chapter 2) and discusses the ways in which computers have been developed to exploit the potential of parallel processing (Chapters 3 and 4).

In the second part we turn to the topic of distributed processing. Included in this is a discussion of what is meant by a fully distributed processing system (Chapter 5), ways of interconnecting computers (Chapter 6) and how a distributed processing system might be designed (Chapter 7).

Part 3 is devoted to the programming of distributed and parallel systems. We look at ways of finding the parallelism which exists in conventional programs (Chapter 8), as well as the ways of developing extra language features to express parallelism implicitly and explicitly. As a particular example we look at the ways in which programs can be developed for an array processor (Chapter 9). The ways in which distributed processes can be synchronized when memory is shared are also discussed (Chapter 10). Hoare's Communicating Sequential Processes model is studied with particular reference to the language occam developed by Inmos (Chapter 11).

The final part takes a look at some possible architectures which may form the basis of the next generation of computers. Ways in which the traditional structure of the von Neumann machine can be replaced by alternatives which more closely reflect new models of computation are discussed. These new models can help us to utilize fully the potential for parallelism which exists in many problems. Three particular approaches are studied: the data flow approach (Chapter 12), the functional approach (Chapter 13) and an approach designed for artificial intelligence — the connection machine (Chapter 14).

A summary of the book together with some thoughts on other developments provides the closing chapter. This is followed by a bibliography which includes all the references made in the 'Further Reading' sections of previous chapters. This bibliography includes all the sources which were used to prepare the original course notes and I would like to acknowledge the contribution made to this book by all the authors concerned. Many of their ideas have been incorporated (sometimes without detailed credit) into the text of this book. In the continual process of revision which the notes have undergone since the course was first given in the session 1980/81, some of the original references to sources and ideas may have been lost. To all those who feel that they have received less credit for their work than they deserve, I apologize in advance. No credit is claimed for the originality of the ideas discussed in this book. Furthermore, some of the examples used have been strongly influenced by those given in the original source texts used in the preparation of the course. I hope, however, that the reader will find the overall presentation of the ideas original and stimulating.

Chapters 12 and 13 contain material I originally prepared for my book on Data Flow Computing published by Ellis Horwood Limited, Chichester, England (1985), and I wish to thank them for allowing me to include it in this text.

Thanks are also due to the students who attended the courses I have given on Distributed and Parallel Processing. Their reactions to the material presented have influenced greatly the contents of this book. Finally, I must thank the publishers for the patience they have shown whilst I have attempted to transform the original course notes into a manuscript in publishable form. Whether I have truly achieved that aim I leave to the reader to judge.

Chapter 1

Introduction

The aim of this book is to introduce the reader to the concepts behind the general area of computer science known as distributed and parallel processing. It is not intended to tell you how to build, or even use, a parallel processor or a distributed computing system. The great variety of systems which exist or can be imagined preclude such an aim.

It will be assumed that the reader has experience of using a variety of computer systems and languages, and has a basic understanding of how computers work.

Before we can discuss in detail the various aspects of distributed and parallel processing systems we need to make sure that we know what we mean by the terms 'distributed', 'parallel' and 'processing'.

Processing

Let us define a **task** as an operation or set of operations which are to be performed, and a **process** as the performance of a task. In computing the terms 'evaluation' or 'execution' are often used instead of 'performance'. Clearly then, the term **processing** means the execution of a task.

We will often talk about **processors** as being those things which carry out tasks. In a computer system this is often taken to be the Arithmetic and Logic Unit (ALU) or the Central Processing Unit (CPU). In modern systems, however, we have the concept of a **virtual machine** or **abstract processor.** In other words, a single piece of hardware may be used as if there were many copies of it, each one executing independently.

So far we have implicitly assumed that a processor (be it real or abstract) executes a single process. This one-to-one correspondence need not hold. For example, it is easy to imagine a single processor executing many processes. This is what happens in any computer which runs a multi-user system. Each user is given the impression that he/she is the sole user of the machine by allowing the single processor to execute each user's process for a short period of time in turn.

It is also possible to envisage a system in which many processors co-operate on the execution of a single process. Any computer system which contains not only a CPU but also a processing unit dedicated to the control of input and output devices may be considered to be a multiple processor machine. This is the case even in small machines. If we regard the running of a program as a task to be performed then clearly this is going to involve some input and output as well as some computation. Therefore we have two processors (the CPU and the peripheral processor) co-operating on the execution of a single process.

As a final comment on processing we should note that not only can we have a single processor executing many processes, and many processors executing a single process, but in the general case we have many processors executing many processes with the number of processors and processes being independent of each other.

Parallel systems

The next concept which we need to clarify is parallelism. Let us imagine two users sitting at two terminals connected to a multi-user computer system. Both users are clearly working in parallel. Indeed there may be times when both users depress a key at the same moment. We can say that the two users are working **simultaneously**.

If we now consider the processing unit in the machine which these users are working on then clearly there is only one processor working at any one time, but there is some sort of parallelism in the sense that both users' jobs are being executed using some form of time-sharing. We will refer to this sort of parallelism — where two (or more) things are happening at the same time, but only one is active at any one instant — as **concurrency**.

Distributed systems

If we wish to talk about a distributed computing system we must have some idea of what can be distributed. First of all, we can envisage a computer system which contains more than one processing unit. In such a system we can talk about the hardware being distributed.

If we imagine a distributed computing system consisting of a number of distinct computers linked together in some way then we can see that three other aspects of processing can be distributed. Firstly, the data used in a task can be distributed around the different machines. Secondly, the data may be processed in a number of different machines; the processing itself is distributed. Finally, the functions of the operating system which control the execution of the task can be distributed.

Therefore, in talking about a distributed computing system we need to be clear about what aspects of the system are distributed (hardware, data, processing, control). We also need to know how much each aspect is distributed. For example, if we consider only the control aspect (the operating system), we need to know whether one processor is in overall control, and the other processors perform subsidiary tasks delegated by this chief processor, or whether each processor which performs some of the control function is equally responsible for making decisions about how the system should behave.

Such variety in what may be distributed, and how much, has led some people to talk about **degrees of distributiveness.** The concept is an important one, but we shall try to avoid the use of such awkward terminology.

Distributed and parallel processing

The final word used in the description of the topic of this book was 'and'. Two questions spring to mind because of this usage.
(1) Does parallel processing imply distributed processing?
(2) Does distributed processing imply parallel processing?

Let us consider three examples. First of all we shall return to our example of two users sitting at terminals using a multi-user system. Is this a parallel processing system, a distributed processing system, both or neither? Some processing is being done in parallel, but if we ignore the human components (the users) then at any one instant of time only one thing is being done at once, so it is not a parallel processing system. On the other hand, can we really ignore the work being done in the terminals where key depressions are interpreted into signals to be sent to the computer? If we regard this as some form of processing then not only is this example a parallel processing system, but it is also a distributed processing system. The processing is distributed between the terminals and the computer!

For our next example we will consider a single stand-alone computer. Within its ALU there is likely to be a parallel adder. Does this make it a parallel processing system? Furthermore, the processing is going to be distributed between various components of the ALU. It is also going to involve the input/output devices and the control unit. Does this make it a distributed processing system? The answer to both questions is intuitively no, but how can we arrive at a definition of distributed and parallel processing which is convincing yet which disallows such systems from being considered?

Before attempting to answer this, let us consider a final example. A room contains a number of personal single-user microcomputers. Each one is being used by a different person. Now clearly things are being done in parallel and the processing which is taking place within that room is distributed between the various microcomputers. On the other hand, no one could seriously consider such a system as either a parallel processing system or a distributed processing system.

As a working definition we will consider a distributed and parallel processing system as one which involves the simultaneous operation of multiple interconnected processors. However, in the chapters which follow, we will not let this definition preclude us from discussing systems which do not fit this definition in all respects.

Why distributed and parallel processing?

Having given a (slightly vague) definition of what we mean by distributed and parallel processing, we will next ask a question which perhaps should have been the first topic to be discussed. Why study distributed and parallel processing? One possible answer would be to list some of the things which it promises to give us. The following list is fairly typical of what has appeared in the literature

(1) High system performance. A distributed and parallel processing system should give the user a fast response and high throughput (by doing things in parallel).
(2) High availability. The existence of a number of components should mean that, even if some of them break down, some should still be available for use.
(3) High reliability. As above, multiple components should imply not only that there is always processing power available, but also if a failure occurs the system should be able to recover or at least the response should deteriorate in a controlled way — **graceful degradation.**
(4) High adaptability. It should be easy to provide incremental growth of a system by adding extra components to a distributed system (since it already consists of a number of components). It should be easy to replace and upgrade individual components (hardware and software) in such a system. Extra functions and capacity should be easily provided by adding components. The whole configuration should be flexible and allow it to be adapted to new uses and circumstances.
(5) Consistent response. Even when temporary overloads occur the system should be able to maintain a good response by distributing the work through the system.
(6) Resource sharing. Users will be able to share expensive resources

Introduction

(e.g. phototypesetters) easily.
(7) Automatic load sharing. Individual users' requirements can be automatically balanced over the distributed system.

All these features (and more) have been claimed for distributed and parallel processing systems, and at first glance this may seem ample justification for their study. Unfortunately, if we looked at any development in computer systems design (either hardware or software) we would find that most (if not all) of the above advantages have been claimed for every development yet proposed.

Even in the early days of computing when many people were unconvinced of the usefulness of computerization, the above list of claims would not have been out of place in the sales literature of the time. Distributed and parallel processing is (yet another) attempt to meet the promise of computing. Have we any reason to believe that it will fare any better than all the earlier ones?

It seems to be the case that the rate of increase in computing power and speed is reaching the limits of what can be achieved using conventional approaches. The size of molecules and the speed of light are becoming limiting factors in chip design. Therefore if we are to achieve the above aims then we must find a new approach.

Many computer sites now possess more than one computer so it seems attractive to connect them together in some way. It is not always practical, or even desirable in some cases, to suggest replacing multiple systems with one larger one. The banking system is such a situation. Each bank wants to retain control of its own machine yet it needs to communicate with other banks to transfer funds. It therefore seems desirable to link the machines together to eliminate the need for human interference in the communication.

Human systems are distributed and parallel processing systems. They consist of individual people working independently to a certain extent but co-operating on the completion of some overall task. It seems likely to be a good idea to follow this model in developing computerized systems.

The final justification for studying distributed and parallel processing may seem rather artificial. People have done research into the possibilities of distributed and parallel processing because it is possible to design and build such systems. In this respect research in this area is rather different from many other developments in computing. Most other developments have arisen because of users' needs or desires. Research into distributed and parallel processing is seen by some as a theoretical development looking for an application.

The potential for distributed and parallel processing systems

We have stated that it is possible to build distributed and parallel processing systems. Such a claim must be justified. We can identify three factors which have made the development of such systems more attractive.

Reduction in cost of data transmission

There are more and more cheap intelligent terminals available which reduce the amount of data which needs to be transmitted. The telephone industry is moving from analogue to digital systems, making available, relatively cheaply, a large network to which we can connect computers. Such large networks allow for the sharing of resources.

Satellite technology is providing us with low-cost bit transmission over large distances, increasing the size of networks, increasing the potential application areas and hence reducing costs since the more people who use a system the less it costs each user (in general).

Improved accessibility of remote computers

Various systems have been developed which make it easier to talk to remote machines. Such systems are Viewdata (Prestel), Teletext, Cable Television with response (CATV) and various network systems (X.25, Ethernet, packet-switching). The number of machines around wanting to talk to other machines is also increasing with the growth of hobbyist computing.

Improved resources accessible

There now exists the capability of providing large on-line storage of the order of 10^{12} bits. Large on-line libraries are available which users would like to be able to access from remote sites.

Efficient software for database management and manipulation, and hardware designed specifically for databases (associative memory) have been developed, as have fast special purpose computers (array processors). Software and terminals are now being designed for naive users, and software is being developed to make distribution transparent. These resources which are now potentially available in a distributed system are much greater than they would have been even only a few years ago.

All these factors make the design of distributed and parallel processing systems possible. Since we are approaching the limits of what can be achieved using conventional approaches, any possible alternative merits study. Furthermore, even if the list of claims for distributed and parallel processing systems does resemble lists which have been produced for earlier developments, it does seem likely that at least some of them may now be achievable.

Summary

In this introductory chapter we have attempted to show how the concept of parallel processing is related to that of distributed processing. We saw that, if we chose to, we could view many existing computer systems as parallel and/or distributed processing systems. An attempt was made, however, to draw a distinction between systems which could be regarded as distributed or parallel, and those which really were and were therefore the subject of this book. This is in many ways an impossible task, but hopefully any confusion remaining will be cleared up as the reader progresses.

The second half of the chapter discussed the motivation for the study of distributed and parallel processing. Many of the advantages claimed for the approach have already been claimed by many other developments, but we saw that there was some reason to believe that with distributed and parallel processing we might actually achieve some of them.

Further reading

A number of books have been written on either distributed processing or parallel processing. As we have discussed, it is difficult to produce a useful definition of these terms so each author tends to discuss a slightly different set of systems. The following chapters are recommended if you feel the need to clarify what is meant by distributed and parallel processing.

Weitzman (1980) presents an overview in Chapter 1 of distributed processing using micro and minicomputers. Some of the topics discussed will be raised in later chapters of this book, but the reader may find this rather more specific discussion useful in attempting to get a feel for the subject.

Sections 1 and 2 of Chapter 1 of Lorin (1980) provide another view of distributed systems. Subsequent sections of this introductory chapter will be covered again later in this text.

A quick browse through the introductory sections of any of the other texts listed in the bibliography may also aid the reader trying to appreciate the scope of this text.

Part 1

Parallel Computers

In this first part we will concentrate on parallel processing systems. Initially, we will consider in more detail the nature of parallelism and look at the effect of interaction on the potential for parallel processing. Chapter 3 presents a brief history of the development of parallel computers and discusses in general terms some of the ways in which the traditional von Neumann architecture has to be modified in order to achieve some speed-up by parallel execution. The final chapter in this part looks in slightly more detail at some specific architectures.

Chapter 2

Parallelism and Interaction

In this chapter we will examine in more detail the concept of parallelism and discuss the various ways in which two (or more) parallel processors can (in principle) interact. In order to do this we shall use a simple analogy. We will consider the case of two secretaries who share an office. Initially we will make the following assumptions
(1) Both secretaries are equally competent.
(2) The office contains two desks.
(3) Each secretary has his/her own typewriter, paper, etc.
(4) There is no communication between the secretaries.

The three components in this model are the tasks to be done (typing letters, etc.), the secretaries themselves and the resources they use (e.g. typewriters). The final element of the model is the time taken to perform a task. We will now consider how we might illustrate the relationship between time and activity within the model.

There are two concepts in this model which are separable; the activity of the secretaries and the progress of their work. We may represent the behaviour of this system diagrammatically as in Fig. 2.1. Figure 2.1a shows the relationship between the secretaries' activity and time. Figure 2.1b shows the relationship between the progress of the work being done by the secretaries and time, assuming each secretary performs a single task during the day.

Tasks and sub-tasks

Both these diagrams imply that there is perfect and continuous parallel processing within this system. One reason for this is the rather general definition of a task which we adopted. If we had defined the work of a secretary more realistically into a number of sub-tasks then we would have introduced some dependency between tasks. Typical sub-tasks could have been: open letter, type memo, check memo. There is an obvious dependency between some of the sub-tasks. This concept of dependency between tasks or sub-tasks is fundamental in the study of parallel systems. A task which is dependent upon another cannot be performed until its predecessor is completed. As a general principle, increasing dependency

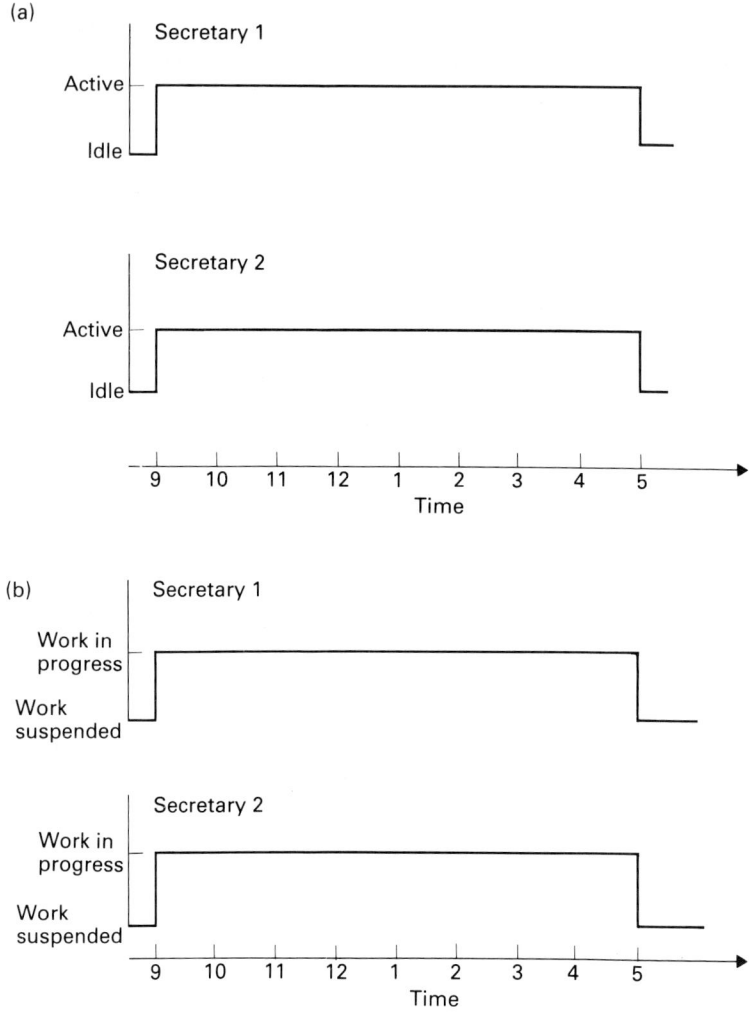

Fig. 2.1 Behaviour of simple two-secretary office. (a) Relationship between the activity of secretaries and time; (b) Relationship between progress of work and time.

decreases concurrency. Figure 2.2 shows the effect of introducing sub-tasks into the work schedule.

The nature of the task we adopt as fundamental in a parallel processing system clearly affects the amount of parallelism which appears to be occurring in a system. Let us now look at the other components of the simple system we have and see if, by changing these only slightly, we can change the way in which the system appears to behave.

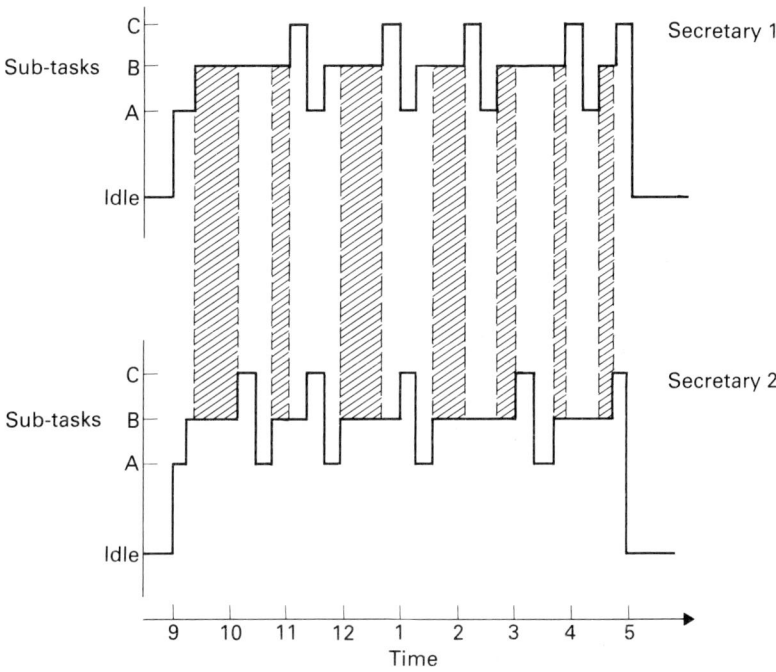

Fig. 2.2 Behaviour of two secretaries with respect to time, showing the effect of introducing three arbitrary sub-tasks. Assuming sub-task B to be the main task (e.g. typing) then full parallel processing (simultaneous typing) only occurs in the cross-hatched regions.

Processors

In the human system we have been looking at, the definition of a processor or secretary remains rather intuitive. Sometimes they behave strictly sequentially, sometimes there is an element of parallelism in their behaviour. We have implied that both secretaries are equally intelligent and capable. If we assumed that one secretary was more capable than the other, then clearly this would have an effect on the behaviour of the system. At the moment we have a **symmetrical** system. If we changed the nature of the secretaries so that one was more capable than the other then we would have an **asymmetric** system.

Resources

In the simple example we are looking at, the resources required are fairly obvious. They would include things such as a typewriter for each secretary, paper, pens, lists of names and addresses and a dictionary. In a computer system the resources required would probably be things such as tape drives, disks, other peripherals and software. One component of the system which may or may not be regarded as a resource is the computer memory. Traditionally this is often considered to be part of the processor in a computer system, but since we can add extra memory it has many of the characteristics which we would associate with a resource.

This question is only of interest when we consider how resources may be added to a system in order to improve its performance. Adding extra memory may or may not be an appropriate option to consider.

When we are considering the provision of resources for a system there are three characteristics which may influence our decision.
(1) Cost. Clearly the cheaper a resource is the more likely we are to be able to provide duplicates of it for multiple processors.
(2) Availability. Having duplicate copies of a resource in a two processor system ensures that the resource is always available (at a price). The need for a resource to be always available depends upon the demand for it. In our simple office analogy the need to provide two typewriters depends on how much typing each secretary is likely to do.
(3) Accessibility. Even if a resource is always available it may not always be easy to access. For example, in a computer system we could keep duplicate copies of some software on tape so that if either of the two processors in a simple dual computer system requires the software then it is available. However, if the tape has to be mounted by an operator then the software is not as accessible as if it was kept on line — on a disk perhaps.

Time

In our simple example we showed the secretaries as working continuously from nine to five. In a more accurate representation we would have to allow for them arriving early or late, leaving early or late and for tea, coffee and lunch breaks. Representing the system taking into account these factors would lead to diagrams such as those in Fig. 2.3. If we took an even finer grain of timing we could regard the secretaries as not working unless they are actually typing or writing a letter, or answering the phone for example.

If we examine their behaviour too critically then we might find that there are very few times in the day when they are both actually working at the same instant. This would imply that there is little, if any, true parallel-

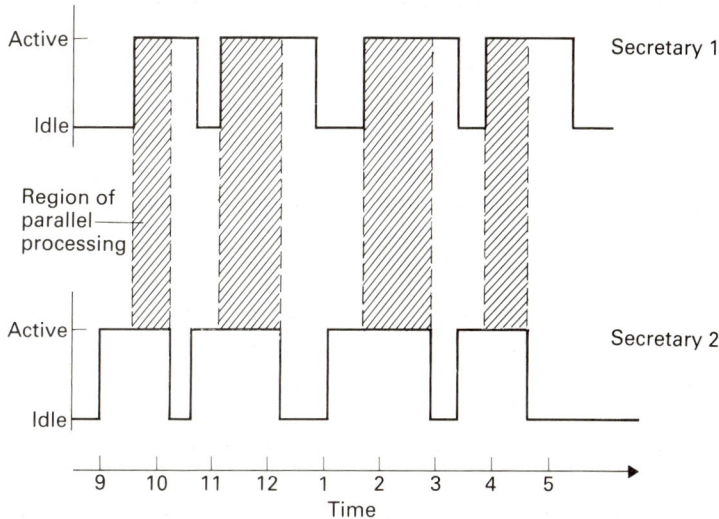

Fig. 2.3 Introducing a finer grain of timing into the secretary model.

ism. This is clearly an unrealistic observation, but it serves to illustrate that we must be careful in our choice of timing values to avoid producing an artificial impression of the degree of parallelism.

Extent of the system

We considered our system to consist of two secretaries. A lot more is happening in the office than the two secretaries working; dust is collecting on the floor, the lights may be working, the secretaries may be smoking, drinking or talking. If we included all these activities within our model we would obtain a false impression of the amount of parallel processing taking place. Once again, we have to be careful to include only the relevant components.

An analogous computer system

Our simple office system is analogous to a computer system consisting of two functionally independent computer systems with all software and files duplicated.

The processors are identical, independent and anonymous (i.e. a user cannot tell which machine he/she is using). Such a system is called a

Symmetric Independent Multicomputer system. Let us consider its performance in relation to a single computer system (assuming that all processors work perfectly). Adding a second processor would
(1) Increase the throughput by a factor of two.
(2) Give an effective degree of parallelism of 100%.
(3) Cost twice as much.

The aim of parallel processing systems may be regarded as trying to achieve as close as possible the first two aims whilst reducing the cost increase to a minimum.

Introducing interaction

The simple model we have used so far assumes that the work for each secretary is completely independent of the work allocated to the other. As a first example of how the interaction in this simple parallel processing system might be increased, we will consider the possibility of both secretaries selecting tasks to be done from a common list. That is, rather than each secretary having his/her own in-tray, we will assume that there is only one (larger) in-tray. When a secretary has finished a task he/she will collect another one from this in-tray.

Such a system may be termed **self-scheduling** as there is no outside influence dictating which secretary selects which task. Furthermore, as we have described it the secretaries merely select another task when they have completed their current one. They do not plan what they are going to do for a whole day at a time. The system may thus be considered to be a **dynamic self-scheduling** system.

Such a scheme gives rise to the possibility of **contention** (i.e. both secretaries may try to select something from the in-tray at the same time). This is illustrated in Fig. 2.4. This problem may be resolved by giving priority to one of the secretaries, as shown in Fig. 2.5. Unfortunately, this means that one of the secretaries might have to be idle whilst waiting for the other to make his/her selection.

In general, introducing interaction into a parallel processing system introduces the possibility of contention. Any method of resolving the contention leads to the possibility of one of the processors being idle for some time, thus reducing the potential increase in throughput and efficiency of adding a processor.

If selecting a task from the in-tray was merely a matter of picking up a piece of paper then the amount of time a secretary may be idle whilst waiting to make his/her selection would be minimal. However, it may be

Parallelism and Interaction

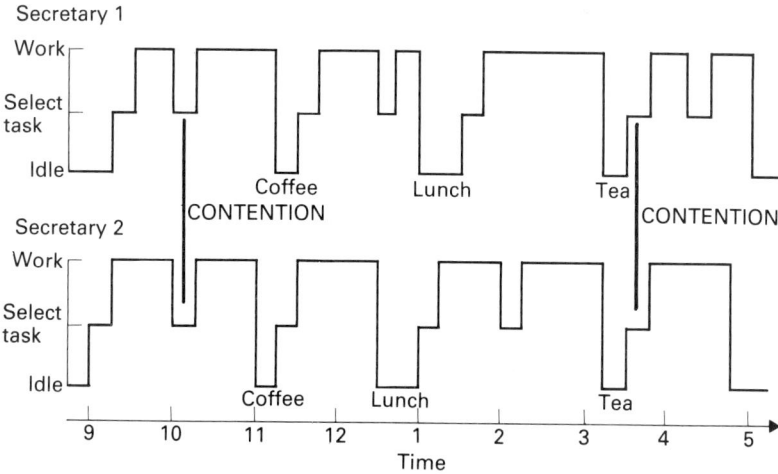

Fig. 2.4 Illustrating how introducing task selection may cause contention.

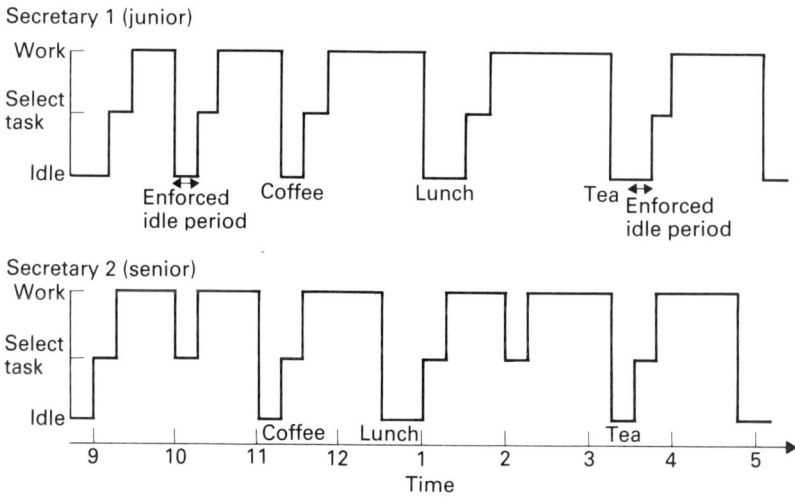

Fig. 2.5 Showing the effect of giving one secretary priority in task selection.

the case that selecting a task is a longer process; perhaps all the appropriate files have to be collected, for example. In this case the time wasted by the waiting secretary may be unacceptably long. A possible solution would be to modify the selection process as below
(1) Choose task.

(2) Mark it as selected.
(3) Collect appropriate files from elsewhere.
(4) Pick up task from in-tray.

Now if we insist that only the first two steps are an uninterruptable task, then the second secretary can begin his/her selection process overlapping with the first one collecting the files. Such a scheme reduces the idle time of the secretaries, but increases the time and effort involved in the selection process. The apparent increase in concurrent processing achieved by adopting this solution is to some extent artificial since the activities being carried out in parallel are those which are made necessary by the introduction of parallel processing.

Interfacing to the outside world

Now let us modify the model to include some interaction between the secretaries and the outside world (their bosses). So far the secretaries have merely selected tasks from a common in-tray, and we have implicitly assumed that any task to be done is totally self-explanatory and can be placed in the in-tray without further communication. Now we wish to introduce the concept of the person who has prepared the task talking to one or other of the secretaries when leaving the task to be done. Since there is no communication between the secretaries, a possible algorithm to allow this to happen would be for one secretary to receive all the tasks on Mondays, Tuesdays and Wednesdays, and the other to receive them on Thursdays and Fridays.

This sort of system probably represents the loosest possible form of coupling between two independent systems. In a computer system a suitable analogy would be a batch processing sytem with two processors which shared a common disk drive on to which jobs (tasks) are placed. Jobs would be input via a card reader, say, which was on-line to one machine on Mondays, Tuesdays and Wednesdays and on-line to the other machine on Thursdays and Fridays.

If we now examine the relative merits of such a system as compared to a single processor system we note the following
(1) Increase in throughput < 2 because of potential contention (probable increase of the order of 1.8).
(2) Increase in cost < 2 because of sharing resources (typical figure might be around 1.6).

The aim is to achieve a cost increase factor less than the performance increase factor. Only when this is true do we appear to have gained

Parallelism and Interaction

anything from adopting a parallel processing system. If we were interested in such factors as increased reliability then parallel processing may give us increased reliability without giving increased performance. With more processors it is increasingly unlikely that we would be left at any time without any processing capability.

Increasing interaction

There are two aspects of the above simple system which can be altered in order to increase the interaction between the two processors (secretaries) and thus produce a more tightly coupled system: the relationship between the secretaries and the sharing of resources.

Looking at the first of these, one possibility is to designate one secretary the senior secretary. It would then seem reasonable to say that the senior secretary would be responsible for accepting and allocating all work. The junior secretary would then have to be able to interrupt the senior one in order to obtain a new task. Two possible scenarios are outlined in Fig. 2.6. In Fig. 2.6a the junior secretary can interrupt the senior one only at times convenient to the senior one. That is only between tasks when the senior secretary is selecting him/herself a new task. The disadvantage of this approach is that the junior secretary may be idle for long periods waiting for the senior secretary to complete a task. The main advantage is that the senior secretary is always busy either performing a task or selecting one for him/herself or the junior.

The alternative strategy is to allow the junior secretary to interrupt the senior one whenever he/she needs a new task. This has the advantage of always keeping the junior secretary busy. The senior secretary is also always busy, but it is likely that he/she will take longer to perform some tasks since he/she will have to recover from any interrruption. Thus, in effect, we are wasting some of the senior secretary's time, and surely, as the senior secretary, his/her time will be more valuable than the junior's. A system in which there is a junior and senior processor is often referred to as a master-slave relationship. If we adopt the latter strategy outlined above it might be reasonable to pose the question — who is the master and who is the slave?

The most likely solution to the above problem, which seems to imply that one secretary is always likely to be wasting time, is to adopt a hybrid solution in which the tasks are divided up into sub-tasks, some of which are interruptable and some of which are not.

We have now arrived at an asymmetric parallel processor system in

20   *Chapter 2*

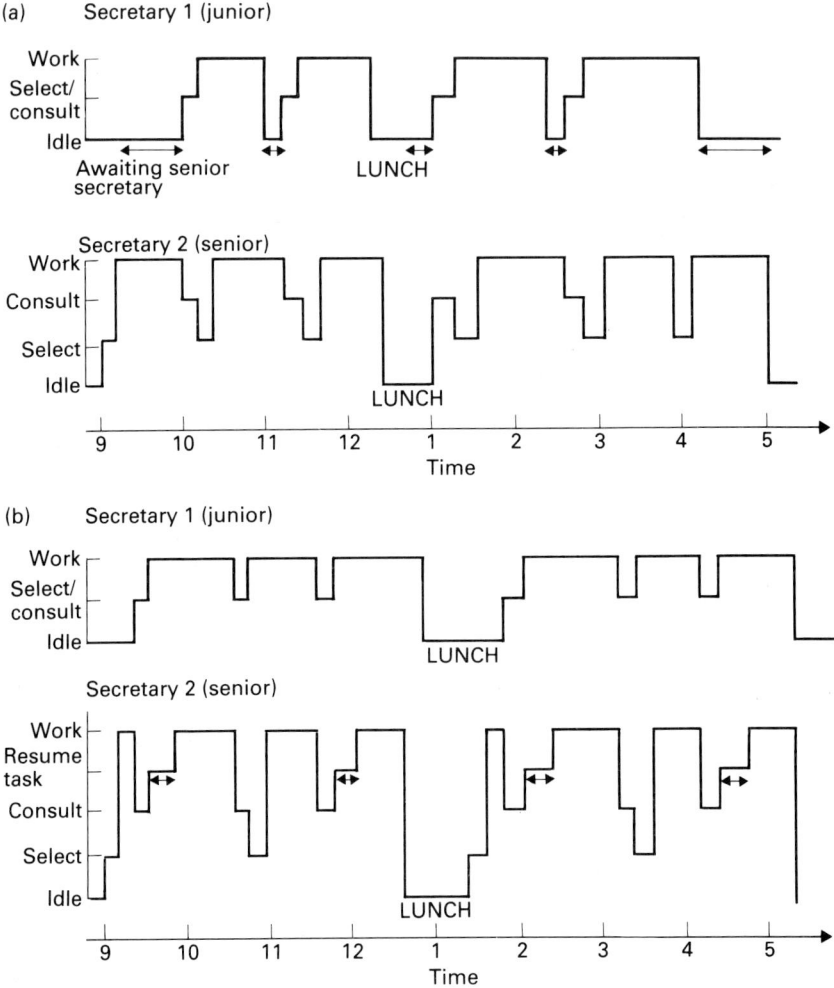

Fig. 2.6 The interaction between two secretaries when only one (the senior secretary) can select tasks. Note that coffee and tea breaks have been omitted. (a) The junior secretary can only consult the senior secretary at times convenient to the senior secretary. Enforced idle time for the junior secretary is indicated thus ⟷ ; (b) The junior secretary can interrupt the senior secretary at any time. Cost of the senior secretary resuming unfinished jobs is shown by the periods indicated thus ⟷ .

which processors have various specializations. The resources of each processor no longer need to be identical. Furthermore, by introducing communication we have introduced the concept of **synchronization.** Some

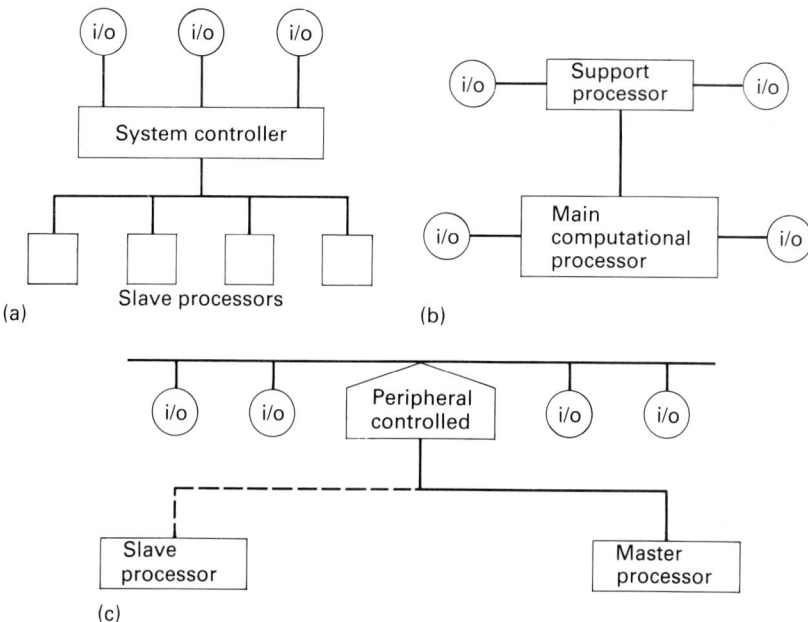

Fig. 2.7 Typical computer system configurations involving co-operative processing. (a) Large system controller backed by computing slaves of less power; (b) Support processor serves main high-power computational processor; (c) Two identical processors (one nominated as master) share common peripherals.

typical computer configurations of this form are shown in Fig. 2.7.

The second aspect of the model which we said we ought to consider was the question of pooled resources. If the total amount of typing both secretaries did in a day was less than one day, then there would be the possibility of sharing a typewriter. Whether any delay would be caused by the sharing of a typewriter would depend upon whether there is ever a time when both secretaries wished to be typing at once and whether jobs could be rescheduled to avoid delay.

When considering shared resources three points need to be considered for each resource
(1) Ownership of resource.
(2) Whether a process may interrupt a user using a resource.
(3) Whether the owner of a resource can pre-empt others for the use of its own resource.

In a computer system, typical shared resources would be memory, channels, control units and peripherals. In general, increased sharing of resources reduces the capital cost of a system, increases the contention and reduces the throughput. Earlier we mentioned software as a resource. A lot of software (including compilers, editors, etc.) can be shared by two or more users. One copy of the software can be executed simultaneously by two or more processors. Therefore, although in some respects we can regard software as a resource, it is a different type of resource than hardware resources.

Summary

In this chapter we have examined very briefly the nature of a simple parallel processing system consisting of two processors. Even with such a simple model we have been able to illustrate some important principles. We saw that increasing dependency decreases concurrency. We also noticed that we have to be careful in our choice of timing values to avoid producing an artificial impression of the degree of parallelism. The same applies to our choice of task definition, and what we decide to include in our definition of a system.

The aim of parallel processing systems may be regarded as trying to increase the available computing power, and the throughput, as much as possible whilst keeping the cost increase to a miminum. Keeping the cost down usually involves the sharing of resources and/or increasing the interaction between the processors. In general, increased sharing of resources reduces the capital cost of a system, increases the contention and reduces the throughput. The possibility of contention is also increased by introducing interaction into a parallel processing system, and any method of resolving the contention leads to the possibility of one of the processors being idle for some time; thus reducing the potential increase in throughput and efficiency of adding a processor.

Further reading

Chapters 1–4 of Lorin (1972) discuss the topics introduced in this chapter in much greater detail. My simple office analogy owes a lot to his repair shop model of a parallel processing system.

Chapter 3
A Brief History of Parallelism

The processing speed of computers has increased dramatically since the 1950s. The increase in the speed of computer arithmetic has been roughly ten-fold every five years. The first generation of computers used valves and had a gate delay of around 1 μs. In the 1960s the second generation used transistors and the gate delay was reduced to around 0.3 μs. With the advent of integrated circuit technology, an average gate delay of about 10 ns in 1965 had been reduced to about 1 ns by 1975. From 1950 to 1975 the speed of components, as measured by gate delay, had increased by a factor of about 1000, whilst the performance, as measured by floating point operations per second (flops), had increased by a factor closer to 100 000. Today people readily talk about machine speeds in terms of Gigaflops (10^9 flops). The Japanese Fifth Generation Computer Project has as its target a machine with a speed of 10 Gflops, whereas the United States Strategic Computing Project demands a machine which can run at a speed of 1 Teraflop (10^{12} flops).

In order to achieve this sort of speed-up we need some form of parallel processing. All such techniques in some sense also distribute the processing. If we equate speed-up with faster response time then for any multi-user system some speed-up can always be achieved by having multiple machines, but in order for such a system to be useful these machines will need to be connected in some way. A set of connected computers is a distributed processing system and we will be looking at such systems later. For the moment we will concentrate on ways of achieving speed-up by modifying the traditional architecture of a single machine.

Architectural speed-up techniques

All the different ways of designing parallel processors involve some form of replication of part of the basic architecture. We can identify four basic levels of replication.

Multiprocessors

The whole of the traditional machine architecture is replicated and the copies interconnected. Communication is usually effected by using some common memory. This is in many ways the ultimate design for parallel processing, since theoretically we have the potential to do anything in parallel which possibly can be done in parallel. It is also the point where parallel processing meets distributed processing. A loosely coupled multiprocessor might be considered a distributed processing system, whereas a tightly coupled distributed processing system might be considered to be a multiprocessor. The concept of coupling will be discussed again later. Essentially the terms tight and loose coupling refer to the speed and bandwidth of communication. Communication via common memory is tight coupling; communication over an asynchronous network is loose coupling.

The main problems with the multiprocessor approach are
(1) The synchronization of the individual processors.
(2) The potentially high cost, in both time and hardware terms, of transmitting data and control information between processors.
(3) The non-trivial task of compiling programs to run efficiently on multiprocessors.

Multifunction processors

Rather than replicate the whole processor, one possibility is to replicate only some function units and expand the control unit in order to allow them to operate in parallel. These units are allowed to operate simultaneously on different data. Often special purpose units, typically for floating point operations, are added in order to increase the speed even further. This approach requires less data and control information to be transmitted between components than the multiprocessor approach, but we have made the system less extensible by being more selective and choosing to replicate specialized functions units.

Array processors

A solution to the synchronization problem of the general multiprocessor is to replicate the processors but retain a common control unit. An array of identical processing units operate simultaneously on separate items of data, but under the control of a single control unit. Each processing unit performs the same task at the same time on different data items. The many problems which require the same operation to be performed on many items of data can be speeded up in this way. This approach is not as limiting

A Brief History of Parallelism

as might appear at first because, given the possibility of performing a single operation on many items of data (an array of data) at once, many problems can be recast in terms of array operations to utilize the parallelism provided. This will be discussed further in Chapter 9.

We are, however, left with the interconnection problem and the architecture is less applicable to general problems.

Pipeline processing

This approach involves replication within the ALU and CPU. An assembly line technique is used with the instruction/execution cycles for consecutive instructions being overlapped. The traditional instruction cycle consists of five phases
(1) Transfer address in SCR to memory unit.
(2) Read from that address to control unit (op-code) and ALU (operand).
(3) Decode the instruction.
(4) Instruct the ALU to perform the operation.
(5) Set the SCR to next instruction.

In the pipeline processor these operations are overlapped. As soon as one instruction has been read, the next one is fetched and decoded, so that as soon as the ALU has finished one operation it can immediately start the next. In many ways this approach is the most economical, but the speed-up depends upon the length of the pipe which in turn depends upon the number of clock cycles each instruction takes to execute. Also, pipeline processors work best on programs which contain long sections of sequential code. Transferring control from one part of a program to another dramatically reduces the speed-up achievable in a pipeline processor.

Figure 3.1 illustrates the relationship between these four approaches and lists some example machines. The architectures are compared in tabular form in Fig. 3.2. All the approaches discussed have their drawbacks and the usefulness of some is limited to specific problem areas. There have therefore been many attempts to combine the different approaches in order to get the 'best' of the basic approaches. The danger in this form of combination processing is that we can end up with the worst characteristics, not the best.

We will now examine briefly the development of each of these approaches to parallel processing. The early electronic computers (EDSAC, EDVAC, UNIVAC 1, etc.) used bit-serial arithmetic. The British ACE and DEUCE designs introduced parallel operation of

Chapter 3

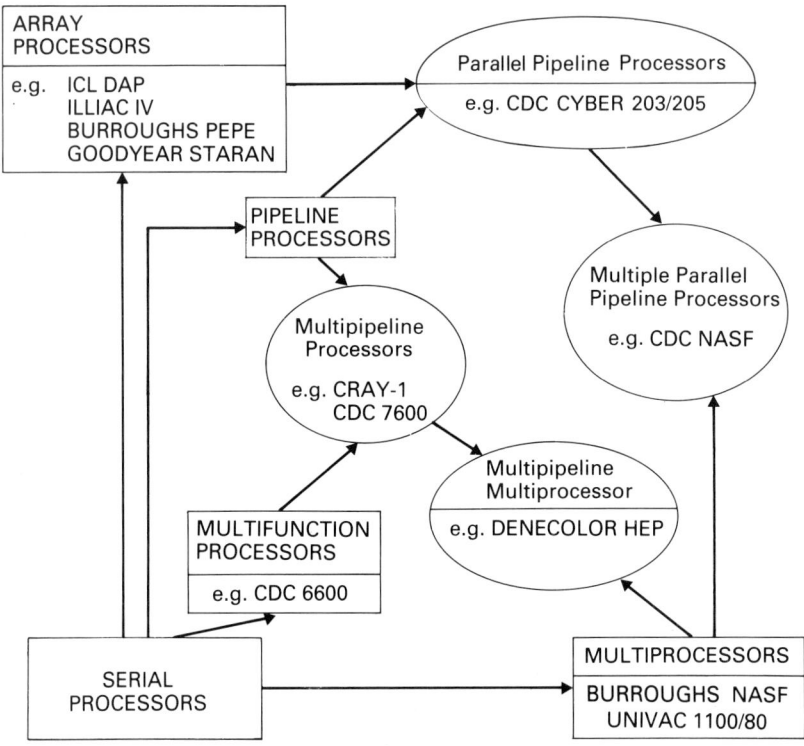

Fig. 3.1 Relationships between architectural speed-up techniques showing some example architectures.

peripherals and also provided vector operations on 32 bits in delay lines. Even in these early days of computing (1951–1954) parallel processing was an important concept.

Bit-parallel arithmetic first appeared in a commercial machine around 1953 with the advent of the IBM 701. Its successor, the IBM 704, was first produced in 1955 with the last one being turned off as late as 1975. The IBM 709, introduced in 1958, added i/o channels in order to increase the throughput. A re-engineered version using transistors was produced in 1959 and called the IBM 7090.

In order to speed up scalar computers, multiple arithmetic units, registers and memory units were added. This was the start of the multifunction approach to parallel processing. The principle of looking ahead to see what could be done in parallel became important. In 1964 the CDC 6600 was the

Speed-up technique / Characteristic	Serial	Pipeline	Array	Multifunction	Multiprocessor
Processing	Serial	Unwind serial	Replicated serial	Replicated functions	Replicated serial
Control unit	Single	Expanded single	Single	Expanded single	Replicated single
Processor interconnections	No	No	Yes	Yes	Yes
Interprocessor synchronization	No	No	No	Yes	Yes
Speed-up potential	1	Limited by pipeline length	Unlimited on many applications	Unlimited on most applications	Unlimited on most applications

Fig. 3.2 Comparison of some basic characteristics of architectural speed-up techniques.

first computer to employ functional parallelism as a major feature. At about the same time IBM developed the STRETCH machine which was marketed briefly as the IBM 7030. This computer had two parallel memory banks and a look-ahead facility to decode and fetch instructions and operands before they were actually needed.

This was the start of the pipelining approach. Perhaps one of the most well-known pipelined computers is the CRAY-1 developed by Seymour Cray after he left CDC in 1972. Essentially, he developed pipelined versions of the original CDC 6600 series. The CRAY-1 was a vector computer operating on 64-bit floating point numbers. CDC's CYBER series now gives a similar performance to the CRAY.

Further development on this line has now been intermingled with the multiprocessor approach, as the limits have been reached on what can be achieved using single processors, no matter how much parallelism could be built in to a single processor.

We will now turn to the array processor approach. Many people associate von Neumann solely with the standard design of a computer, but back in 1952 he presented a design for an array of processors. Unger's design of 1958 was one of the first practical design proposals.

The SOLOMON (Simultaneous Operation Linked Ordinal MOdular Network) design of 1962 proposed a two-dimensional 32 × 32 array of processing elements each with 128 32-bit memory, and a bit-serial ALU under the control of a single control unit. This approach to parallel processing was fundamentally different from the vector pipeline development of serial computers. The SOLOMON machine was never actually built but it did give rise to the ILLIAC IV and Burrough's PEPE floating point array processors.

Two other array processors, the Goodyear Aerospace STARAN and the ICL Distributed Array Processor (DAP), used arrays of 1-bit processors. Conventional machines manipulate data in units called words (anything from 8 bits in the smaller microcomputers to 60 bits in CDC 6000 and 7000 series machines). They are thus word-serial bit-parallel machines. An alternative approach is to address the same bit in all memory words at the same time (word-parallel bit-serial). Such machines are often referred to as **orthogonal** computers, or **associative** processors. Sanders Associates produced one of the first commercial orthogonal computers known as the OMEN (Orthogonal Mini EmbedmeNt) in the early 1970s.

Turning now to the multiprocessor approach. This might be considered to have been started in 1959 when Holland made a proposal for a parallel processor with each processor having its own instruction stream. A typical early 1960s design was the Burroughs D-825 which consisted of four processors connected using a crossbar network. We have already mentioned the CDC 6600 in our discussion of pipelined computers. In the late 1960s CDC introduced the 7600 which was basically a dual processor version of the 6600 using solid state memory.

The 1970s saw an increased interest in multiprocessors, both by research institutions and by major manufacturers. The Univac 1100/80 produced in the mid-1970s was a four-processor design with shared resources. Around 1980, IBM produced the 308X which consisted of either two or four processors arranged symmetrically. All these examples use only a handful of processors at most. Even the Cray X-MP which many people consider to be state of the art multiprocessor supercomputer technology uses a maximum of only four processors.

Academic developments in multiprocessors tended to use many more processing units. One of the first major designs was Carnegie-Mellon's C.mmp project which linked 16 PDP-11s together using a crossbar and connected memory. The successor to this project is the $C.m^*$ research vehicle for studying hierarchically structured processor clusters. This is aimed at allowing large numbers of processors to be connected together.

The C.mmp approach used a crossbar connection mechanism; an alternative approach is the use of direct shared memory, as used in the

CYBA-M project.

Another multiprocessor which is available today and uses 16 processors is the HEP multiprocessor from Denecolor. This is another shared memory design with the processors being connected to the memory via a packet switched network.

Other designs currently under development include the S-1 project at Lawrence Livermore which consists of 16 processors sharing memory via a crossbar switch, the ETA/GF-10 design which consists of eight Cyber-205 processors linked together and the Cedar project where between 16 and 256 processors are to be linked with a hierarchical control structure.

Intel have recently announced their so-called 'Personal Supercomputer' which is based on CalTech's hypercube of 128 IBM pcs. The speed of this design is said to be around 12 Mflops.

Another interesting development is the INMOS transputer which is a simple uniprocessor. Nevertheless, it deserves a mention in this chapter as it is designed to be used as a building block in multiprocessors consisting of a very large number of processors.

In the next chapter we will be outlining in more detail the actual designs of some of the machines mentioned in this brief history, in an attempt to illustrate some of the different approaches which have been taken.

Summary

We have summarized very briefly some of the major developments in parallel computer design, showing how the three initial approaches of array processors, pipelining and replication of functional units are all approaching the limits of their evolution. Most major work is now being done on multiprocessors. Figure 3.3 shows the historical development of a selection of parallel computers from the early 1950s to the mid-1980s. It also gives an indication of the relative speeds of the designs.

Further reading

Rather than give a long list of original reports on all the various designs mentioned, the reader is advised to start with Section 1.1 of Hockney & Jesshope (1981). This section provided the basis for the original set of notes for this part of my course. Subsequent developments can be found summarized in various papers including those in the June 1985 issue of the IEEE's *Computer* magazine (IEEE 1985). Chapter 15 of Chambers *et al.* (1984) provides a brief introduction to closely coupled architecture. In

30 Chapter 3

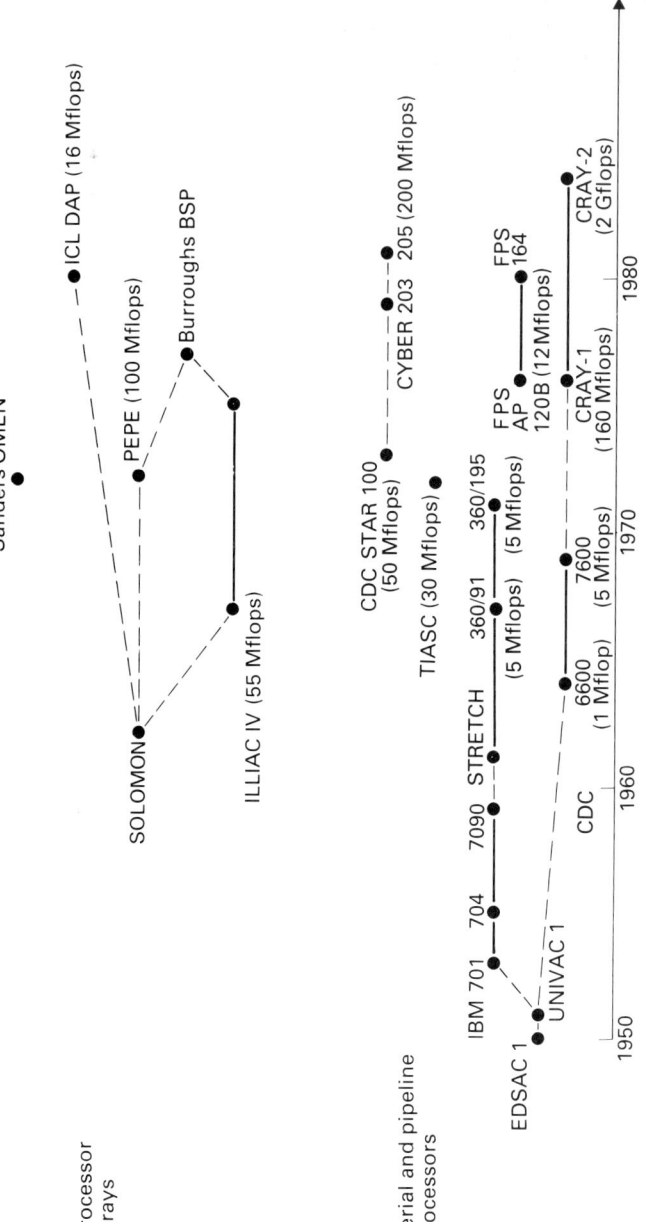

Fig. 3.3 Development paths of some supercomputers indicating dates of first deliveries and approximate speeds.

Evans (1982), Kuck discusses the various ways of modifying the basic architectures of computers in order to achieve speed-up. A final source of information worth mentioning is the excellent survey article by Jean-Loup Baer (1984) on the state of the art of Computer Architecture design.

Chapter 4

Parallel Architectures

In this chapter we intend to illustrate briefly some of the different types of parallel architectures by studying a few example designs. In order to make a meaningful choice of example designs we need to make some attempt to classify the different types of architecture which are possible. One way of grouping similar architectures together is by looking at the different levels within a parallel processing system at which parallelism can occur.

Levels of parallelism

The highest level at which parallel processing can occur is the **job level.** Job level concurrency occurs in any multiprogrammed system when multiple jobs are executed concurrently using time-sharing. True job level parallelism (i.e. simultaneous processing) can occur in any system with multiple processors. A task or job is allocated to a separate processor. Clearly this level of parallelism is closely associated with multiprocessor systems. One question which has to be asked is what is meant by a job or task. The obvious answer is to say that we mean a whole program, but clearly there are cases when it would be more appropriate to consider phases of a job. Thus the dividing line between this level of parallelism and the next is not always an easy one to draw.

The next 'lower' level of parallelism is that of parallel processing at the **program level.** This is usually taken to mean that procedures or subroutines can be executed in parallel. We can also include in this level parallel processing of separate invocations of the body of loops. Frequently, subsequent iterations of a loop can be executed in parallel with earlier ones if there is no dependency between them. Multifunction processors and array processors can provide parallel execution at this level.

In program level parallelism each individual instruction is executed on a single processor. It is clearly possible to envisage **instruction level** parallelism where some parallel processing occurs between phases of an individual instruction. Pipeline processing is an example of this level of parallel processing.

The final level at which parallel processing can occur is the **arithmetic** or **bit level.** The simple parallel adder which many computers use is an

Parallel Architectures

example of this level of parallelism. Normally though, this would not be considered to be of primary interest in the study of parallel processing and we would probably restrict our attention to vector or array instruction parallelism.

Classification schemes

Using the above approach to classify parallel architectures would lead to a grouping similar to that suggested by the four approaches to parallel architecture design mentioned in the previous chapter (multiprocessor, multifunction, array processor and pipelined processors).

An alternative classification proposed by Flynn was to examine the relationship between the instructions a machine receives and the data it manipulates. Flynn's classification relies upon the concept of a **stream.** The stream consists of a number of items. It may be a stream of instructions or a stream of data. Flynn's classification scheme is summarized in Fig. 4.1. The

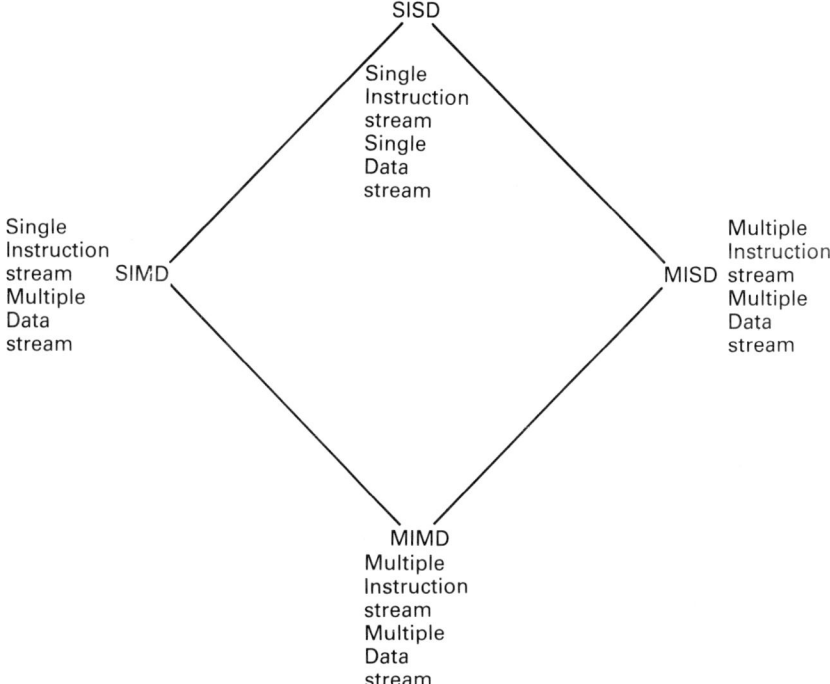

Fig. 4.1 Flynn's classification of computer architecture according to instruction and data streams.

standard computer we are all used to accepts a single stream of instructions each of which acts upon a single stream of data items. Thus such a machine is classified as an SISD machine. Even machines such as the CDC 6600 which involve some parallel processing (pipelining) come into this category.

The diagonally opposite classification, MIMD, represents true multiprocessors where each processor accepts its own instruction stream and acts upon a separate stream of data. The other two possibilities are SIMD, which consists of a single control unit and processors carrying out the same instructions on many items of data (array processors for example), and the theoretically possible MISD machine which would seem to imply that a set of different instructions would all be performed on the same data item. Not surprisingly this category has not received a great deal of attention.

As we mentioned earlier, the four approaches to parallelism outlined in the previous chapter would provide a means of classifying parallel computers. One type could be the standard sequential machine. Even here, two alternatives are possible: bit-serial and bit-parallel machines. Bit-parallel computers would still process words in a sequential fashion. We noted in the last chapter that an alternative approach is that adopted by some array processors of working in a word-parallel bit-serial fashion. This approach was incorporated into a classification scheme proposed by Shore (see Fig. 4.2). Shore's scheme classifies machines according to how they are organized from four basic parts — the control unit, the processor unit, the data memory and the instruction memory. These basic components are regarded as logical and not physical units. For example, although the scheme distinguishes between the instruction memory and the data memory, a single physical memory unit may be used to store both instructions and data.

Machine Type I (see Fig. 4.2a) represents a word-serial bit-parallel architecture. The processor unit may contain multiple function units and may be pipelined. This type is considered to represent the most basic form of sequential computer design. In fact the very first electronic computer designs used bit-serial architectures. By excluding these from the classification system Shore implied that they were out of date. It is interesting to note, though, that some of today's array processors require the use of bit-serial processing techniques.

Word-parallel bit-serial machines are classed as Type II (see Fig. 4.2b). In machines of Type I the processing unit is referred to as a horizontal processing unit. Type II machines are said to have a vertical processing unit. Machines of Type III (Fig. 4.2c) combine these and have two (logical)

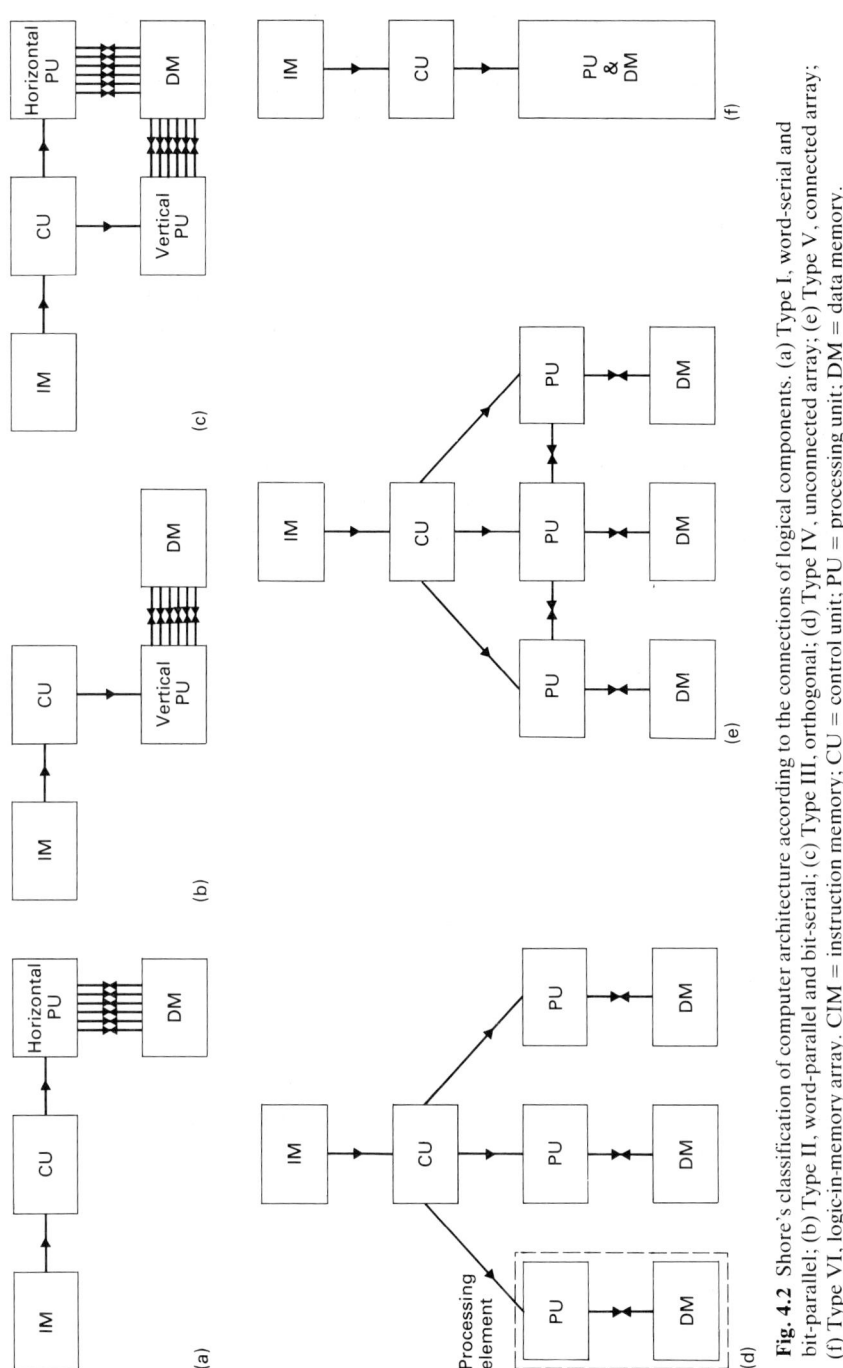

Fig. 4.2 Shore's classification of computer architecture according to the connections of logical components. (a) Type I, word-serial and bit-parallel; (b) Type II, word-parallel and bit-serial; (c) Type III, orthogonal; (d) Type IV, unconnected array; (e) Type V, connected array; (f) Type VI, logic-in-memory array. CIM = instruction memory; CU = control unit; PU = processing unit; DM = data memory.

processing units — one vertical and one horizontal.

Machine Types IV, V and VI are all array processors. Type IV machines consist of an unconnected array of processing unit and data memory pairs (often called processing elements) with a common control unit. This approach is easily extensible but is only useful for a limited range of applications. Machines of Type V (Fig. 4.2e) are similar to Type IV except that some connections are added between neighbouring processing elements. For example, the ILLIAC IV machine provides short-cut communication between every eight processing elements.

Machine Types I to V maintain separate data memories and processing units with some form of data bus or switching element between them. Type VI, illustrated in Fig. 4.2f, is an alternative approach where this separation is not maintained; the processing logic is distributed throughout the memory as in associative processors. Machines of this class are sometimes termed logic-in-memory arrays.

The merits of the classification schemes

None of the above classification schemes are ideal. Flynn's approach gives us some useful broad groupings but tends to group all parallel processors, except multiprocessors, into the SIMD class. It fails to distinguish between pipelined computers and processor arrays which have totally different characteristics. Furthermore, some confusion can arise in the definition of the data stream. For example, a pipelined vector machine can be classified as any of the four possible groups: it may be classed as SISD because it processes a single stream of vector data; it may be classified as SIMD if every element of the vectors is regarded as belonging to an individual stream of data; if we regard the pipelined ALU as operating many instructions in parallel then it may be classified either as MISD or MIMD.

Usually, an SIMD machine is taken to be an array of processors operating under a central control (array processor) and an MIMD machine is taken to be an array of processors each obeying its own instruction stream.

One way of improving Flynn's approach is to subdivide the MIMD category into two classes depending upon whether the processors operate on single data items (scalar values) or upon a vector or array of data. In Chapter 8, when we discuss the different ways in which we can compile programs to be executed on parallel processors this distinction will prove useful. Four possible machine classes can be defined using this type of distinction

(1) SES — single processor executing operations on scalar data (the same as Flynn's SISD).
(2) SEA — single processor executing operations on array data (the same as Flynn's SIMD).
(3) MES — multiple processors executing operations on scalar data (a sub-class of Flynn's MIMD).
(4) MEA — multiple processors executing operations on array data (another sub-class of Flynn's MIMD).

Note that there is no immediate equivalent of the MISD group, though it could be argued that the MES class includes this group.

In his scheme, Shore provides an equivalent class to SISD in his Type I. Types II and V are useful sub-divisions of SIMD. Unfortunately his numbering scheme is fairly arbitrary and he does not deal with multi-processors successfully.

Neither Shore nor Flynn manages to classify multicomputer and multi-processor systems satisfactorily. A multicomputer system may be seen as any system involving two or more computers which are coupled in some way. The loosest form of coupling is illustrated by the use of stand-alone peripheral controllers as shown in Fig. 4.3. Normally we would actually require some electrical or hardware coupling and the loosest form of coupling which satisfies this criteria is the indirectly coupled system shown in Fig. 4.4a. Figure 4.4b shows two possible directly coupled architectures. This type of coupling is also termed tight coupling.

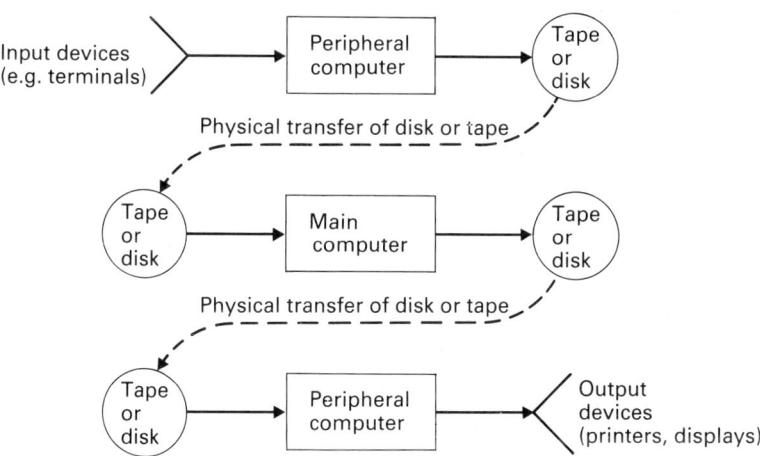

Fig. 4.3 Peripheral stand-alone computer system (loosest possible coupling).

38   *Chapter 4*

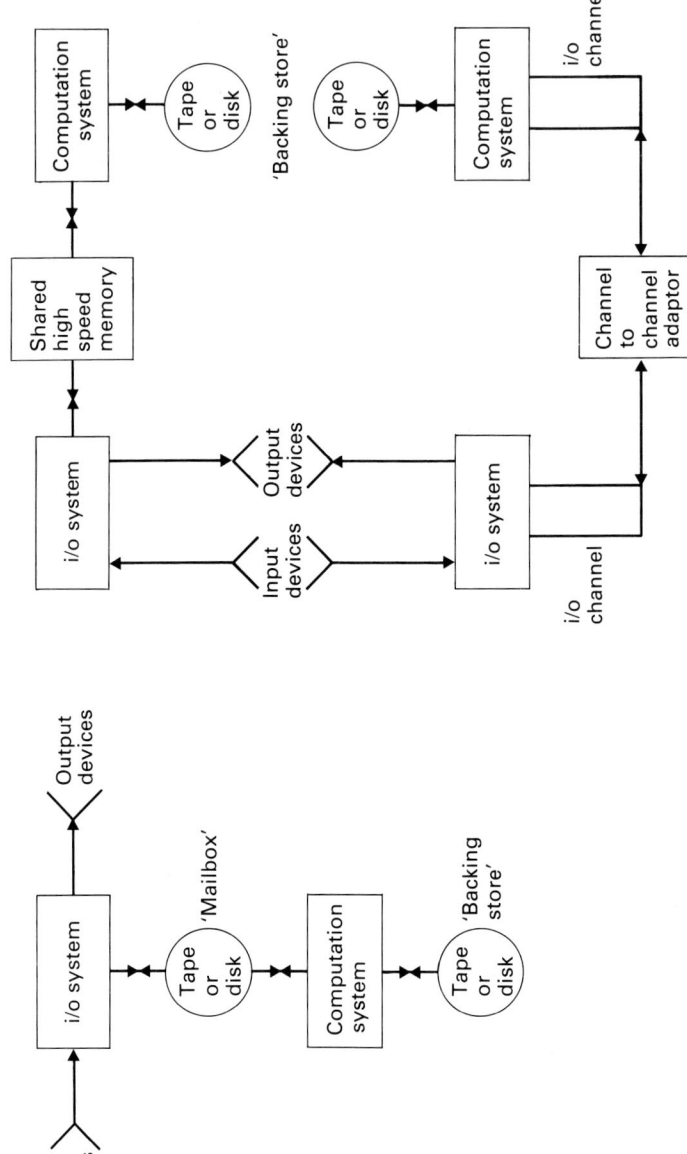

Fig. 4.4 Extreme degrees of coupling in multicomputer systems. (a) Indirectly coupled multicomputer system; (b) Directly coupled multicomputer system.

Multiple computer systems consist of coupled sets of computers which have the potential for operating independently. A multiprocessor system on the other hand usually consists of a number of processors which would not be capable of operating totally independently in the same way.

A definition of a multiprocessor system which was suggested by the American National Standards Institute was that it is

'a computer system employing two or more processor units under integrated control.'

We need to look at this definition in more detail.

If there are two or more processing units some definitions require them to be identical. That is, they only allow symmetric multiprocessor systems. It is clearly possible to envisage designs for asymmetric multiprocessor systems though such systems tend to be less easy to expand.

It is often regarded as essential that processing units share some main memory which is accessible to all processors. One could insist that all main memory is shared, though realistically this is often either impractical or undesirable. Some sharing of i/o peripherals is often regarded as a desirable feature in a multiprocessor system.

The concept of integrated control usually leads to the requirement for a single operating system in overall control of all hardware and software levels. There must be intimate interaction possible at both hardware and software levels (that is within the system software and programs) and at hardware interrupt level.

Some examples of architecture designs

In the rest of this chapter we will look at some specific architectures in order to illustrate some of the approaches taken. We will concentrate on two approaches — array processors and multiprocessors. Discussion of the design of pipeline processors and the use of multifunction units is probably more appropriately left to books on hardware design.

The array processor approach

The classic array processor design can be illustrated by looking at one of the earliest such designs, the ILLIAC IV (see Fig. 4.5). The main components of the system are

(1) A single control unit issuing the same instruction to all the processing elements (PEs) simultaneously.
(2) A set of processors — in the ILLIAC IV there were 64 PEs, each with its own memory.

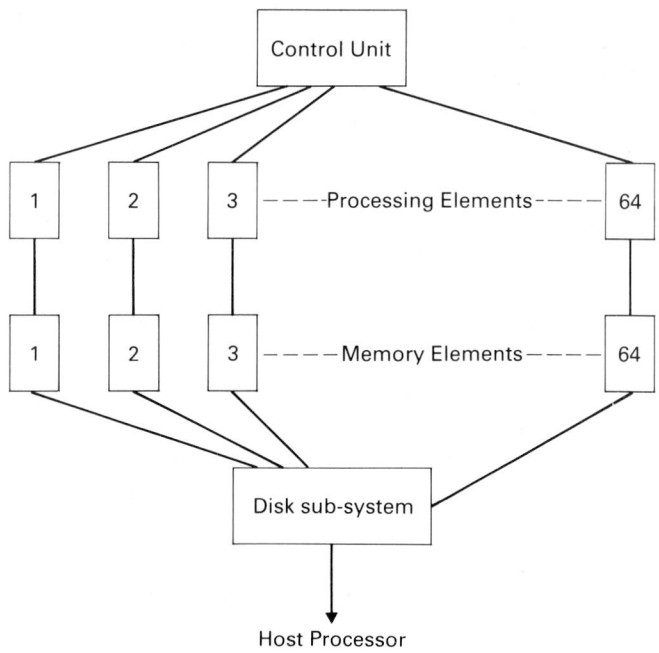

Fig. 4.5 Overview of the structure of the ILLIAC IV computer.

(3) A system for communication between processors and external data sources — in the ILLIAC IV a disk sub-system was used, which was clearly a limiting factor in terms of speed of communication.

We can identify five main ways in which the basic array processor design can be modified.

Firstly, we can change the number of PEs used. A typical application of an array processor is often quoted as being the solution of large meshes in finite difference methods. Such meshes can easily be of the order of 100 × 100 elements (even if we restrict ourselves to two dimensions). The idea of using an array processor is to use a PE per element of the mesh. This implies that we should be thinking of arrays of hundreds of thousands of PEs. Clearly the ILLIAC IV's 64 elements were a long way off this. Other array processor designs have significantly increased the number of PEs.

One factor limiting the number of PEs we can have is their size and cost. This is strongly influenced by the second characteristic of array processors which can vary from implementation to implementation — the complexity of operations supported by the individual PE. An extreme

Parallel Architectures

example of a simple PE is the ICL DAP which uses 1-bit processors.

The number of PEs can also influence the choice of interconnection pattern. We noted in the ILLIAC design that a disk sub-system was used, and that this would be a limiting factor in terms of speed of communication. This is the third factor which distinguishes different array processor designs.

The fourth factor is the size of memory module associated with each PE. Again this can influence the number of PEs it is practical to include in the architecture.

The final characteristic which can vary from design to design is the method of communication with an external system. All practical array processors so far have been designed to work in conjunction with a host processor which downloads sub-programs to the array processor. This is a recognition of the fact that array processors are only really suited to particular applications and are not in general efficient processors for general purpose programming.

Having introduced the basic design of an array processor we will now concentrate on one design in particular, the ICL DAP, partly because in

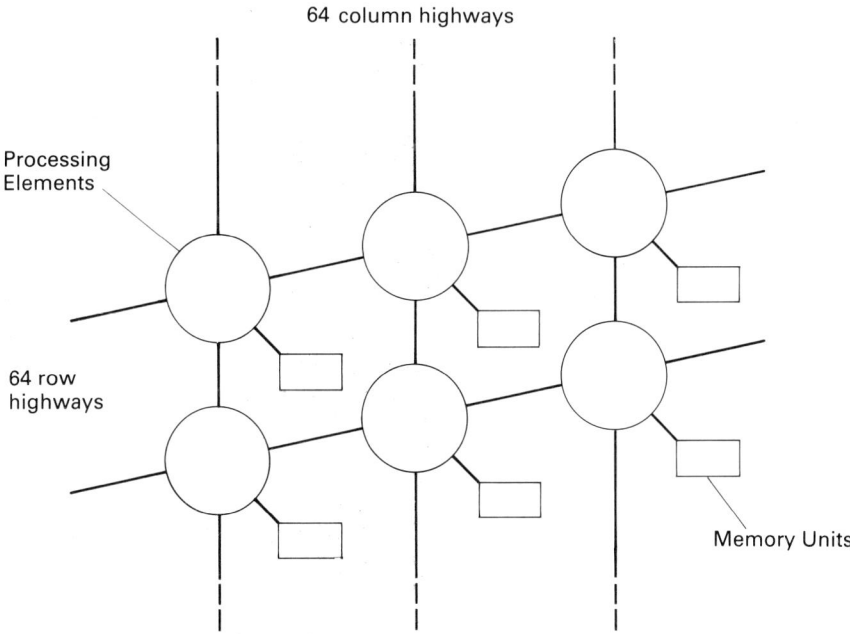

Fig. 4.6 Overview of the structure of the ICL DAP computer.

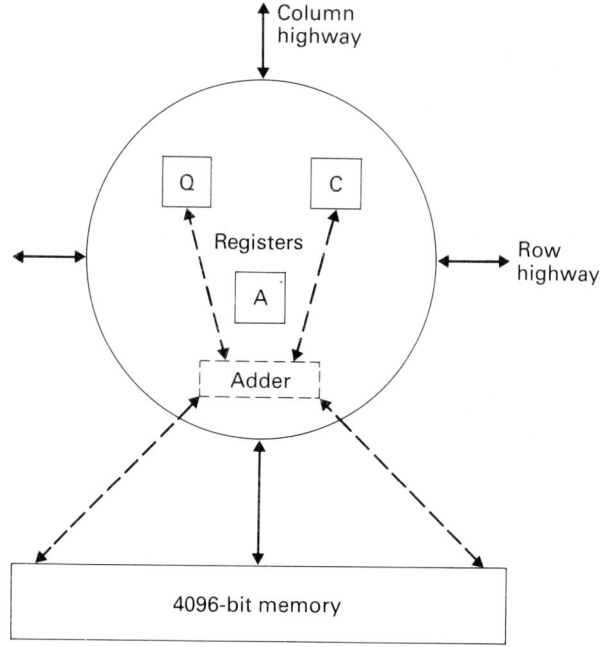

Fig. 4.7 An ICL DAP processing element (PE) with memory.

some ways the design is an extreme example of how a very simple PE can be used. The structure of the ICL DAP is shown in Fig. 4.6. It consists of a two-dimensional array of 64 × 64 PEs. It is easy to envisage how the design could be extended to say 128 × 128 elements. Powers of two are chosen for the sizes as this eases the addressing problem.

Each PE is a 1-bit processor together with a 4096-bit memory (see Fig. 4.7). The PE has three registers, Q, C and A. The only operation it can perform is to add the contents of Q, C and 1 bit of memory, leaving the result in Q and C (C is the most significant — carry-bit). The A (activation) register can be used to indicate whether or not a particular PE is taking part in a particular computation.

A consequence of the 1-bit nature of the processors is that if we consider such a simple operation as addition we require three memory access cycles per unit of precision. This can be seen by looking at the following simple algorithm

```
carry := 0;
for i:=1 to 16
   do    z[i] := x[i] + y[i] + carry;
         if overflow
         then carry := 1
         else carry := 0
   od .   fi
```

This gives us some interesting comparative performance figures for different arithmetic operations as we can see from the list of relative performance figures below

1 bit boolean operation	1
16 bit fixed point addition	10
16 bit data movement	6
32 bit fixed point addition	20
32 bit floating point addition	180
32 bit floating point multiplication	280
32 bit floating point square root	250
64 bit floating point multiplication	1000

A number of points are worth noting
(1) Fixed point arithmetic is usually much faster than floating point arithmetic.
(2) Short precision arithmetic is faster than long precision arithmetic. (For addition and data movement the time is proportional to the number of bits. For multiplication and division the time is proportional to the square of the number of bits.)
(3) Data movement is fast compared to floating point arithmetic.
(4) Logical operations are very fast compared to arithmetic operations.
(5) The relative magnitude of various operations is very different to that observed on conventional word-based hardware; especially word-based floating point hardware.

The main reason for these unusual figures is that the basic PEs in the DAP are relatively slow. The crucial speed parameter is the memory cycle time (minimum elapsed time between successive accesses). This is often three or four times longer than typical times for high performance chips (around 50 ns).

The ICL DAP design can be considered to be a blueprint for any sized two-dimensional array of PEs. In what follows we will assume a 64 × 64 array of processors such as that installed at Queen Mary College, London. There is a single instruction stream coming from a Master Control Unit.

Chapter 4

This unit has eight 64-bit registers connected to row and column highways (see Fig. 4.6). They are used to select/transmit data from/to all processors in a row or column. Data is transmitted simultaneously to all processors by row or by column. For output each processor may AND some data on to a highway. This allows for global enquiries.

To conclude our discussion of the organization of the DAP we must indicate how it is used to interact with the outside world. Each of the 64 × 64 processing elements has 4096 bits of storage. This can be viewed as a cuboid of store of size (64 × 64 × 4096) 2 Mbytes. This is connected to the store highway of an ICL 2980 so that it can address the store as part of its own address space. The operating system just views this area as store having rather special properties and loader routines load the appropriate values into it. This is a similar view to that required for input/output ports which are taken as part of the address space of a machine.

If we consider the three main characteristics of the ICL design to be its very simple PE design, its two-dimensional connectivity and its i/o connections, let us consider what happens if these are changed in some way.

One way of trying to improve performance might be to have a more powerful PE. The French PROPAL-2 design uses a 16-bit based PE (see Fig. 4.8). We have a 1-bit activity register (D), a 16-bit working register (A), and an 8-bit shift register to improve multiplication performance. For bit machines the number of elementary operations for multiplication is proportional to the square of n the number of bits. With an 8-bit shift we

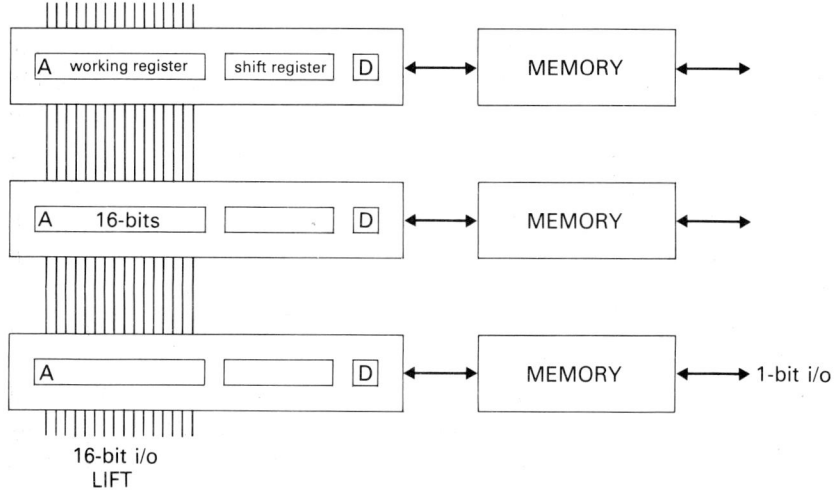

Fig. 4.8 Overview of the design of the PROPAL-2.

Parallel Architectures 45

can reduce that to n times the number of 8-bit units.

Comparing addition and multiplication speeds for the DAP and the PROPAL gives us

mult/add (P) : mult/add (DAP) approx equal 1:8

The other aspect of the design of the array processor which we want to look at is the processor connectivity. Programming any SIMD machine requires data communication between processors. This takes time. Time attributable to data rearrangement can be termed **routing time.** Routing time is proportional to the number of intermediate processors and the bandwidth of the connection. In the ICL DAP the maximum number of intermediate processors is 125 (63 + 62) for a 64 × 64 array of 4096 processors. This figure is quite low. Unfortunately the bandwidth is very low (1 bit) which would tend to increase the time.

In the PROPAL design, processors are connected in a ring with a 16-bit communication 'lift'. A design with 1024 processors would give a maximum number of intermediate processors as 512. If the data transfer time between processors was the same for the two machines, the DAP transfer of 16 bits of information would take a maximum of 125 * 16 transfer cycles (2000), compared with 512 cycles for the PROPAL. A typical cycle time would be around 150 ns for the PROPAL. Therefore the maximum transfer time would be 512*150 = 76.8 µs. This compares with 16-bit multiplication time of around say 20 µs. Since this is the worst case it is true to say that in most algorithms routing time will not dominate.

The DAP approach of increasing connectivity is one way of improving routing time. If the connections were 16 bits wide then we would have 125 transfer cycles compared to 512 for the PROPAL (2 × $\sqrt{N}$ compared to $N/2$). The DAP has two dimensions of connectivity; the next step is three or four dimensions. Following this approach does improve the routing time performance (particularly for larger numbers of processors), but the problem is a physical one of making connections to processors. Two-dimensional connectivity requires connections to four neighbours (2 × 2); three-dimensional connectivity would imply six (2 × 3) neighbours. For 16-bit connections we would need 64 and 96 connections respectively.

We have suggested that routing time is unlikely to dominate, but consider a typical array processor application (matrix multiply). Assuming N^3 processors we require one multiplication, log N additions and $O(N)$ routing steps. This suggests that routing time will dominate. We therefore need fast routing compared to arithmetic. In the PROPAL design this is achieved by having slow arithmetic. One commonly made suggestion for improving the performance of bit-organized parallel processors is the replacement of slow PEs by more powerful ones (e.g. 8-bit microprocessors). This just does not work unless you can significantly improve the routing time. This brings us to a final comment about performance measurement. An oft-quoted figure is the Mflop rate of processors. Unfortunately, even if we took something like the IBM 370 and assumed a floating point multiply time of zero, throughput would only increase by about 10% for the average job. Measurements of flops is great so long as all you ever want to do is floating point operations. In most applications there is at least a significant proportion of data movement and non-floating point operations. Therefore, whilst it cannot be denied that machines with higher flop rates will in many cases give an increase in speed, the increase obtained is nowhere near what you might expect.

A multiprocessor design

Most multiprocessor designs use shared variables for communication between processors (see Fig. 4.9). One of the most interesting recent developments in the field of multiprocessors is the Cosmic Cube design developed at CalTech. This design is based on the use of a message-passing protocol for communication (Fig. 4.10). The connection scheme used is known as a hypercube. In two dimensions we can imagine four (2^2)

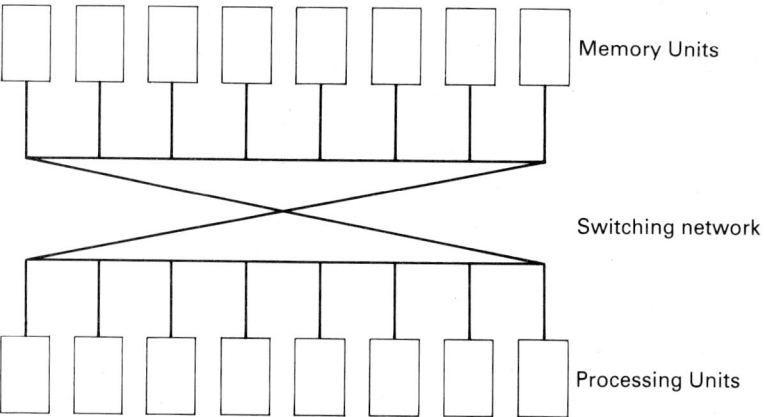

Fig. 4.9 Typical shared memory multiprocessor using a switching network for communication.

Parallel Architectures

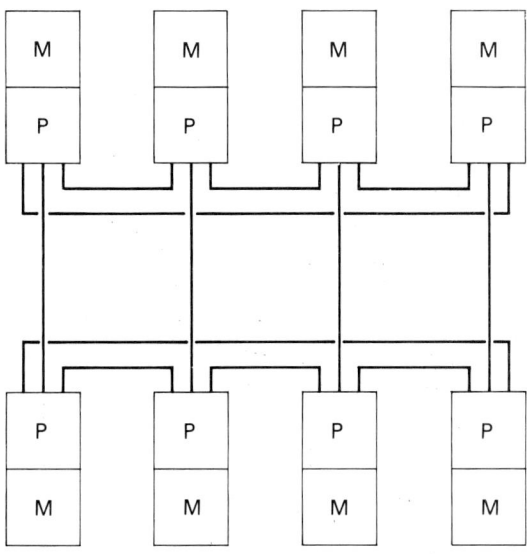

Fig. 4.10 Typical message-passing multicomputer. Architecture is simply three-dimensional cube with each processor connected to three neighbours. P = processing units; M = memory units.

processors each having two neighbours. In three dimensions eight (2^3) processors each have three neighbours. In six dimensions we have 64 (2^6) processors each with six neighbours. The connection pattern is shown in Fig. 4.11 (projected on to two dimensions!). Each node in the hypercube represents a physical processor, at present an Intel 8086 with floating point co-processor (8087). The design is not limited by the choice of processor and in a final production version one could expect purpose built single chip processors to be used.

An important feature of the design is that the large number of connection paths through the processor make it possible for the programmer to virtually ignore the physical structure of the machine and work with virtual processes which are mapped on to the hardware by the operating system. All processes execute concurrently and have a global process ID which serves as its address. Messages are then sent with headers containing the addresses of the destination process and the sending process. Messages are routed around the network and can be queued during transit. It is important, though, that the order of the messages between two processes is preserved. Otherwise rather unpredictable results could be produced.

Many multiprogramming operating systems have been developed

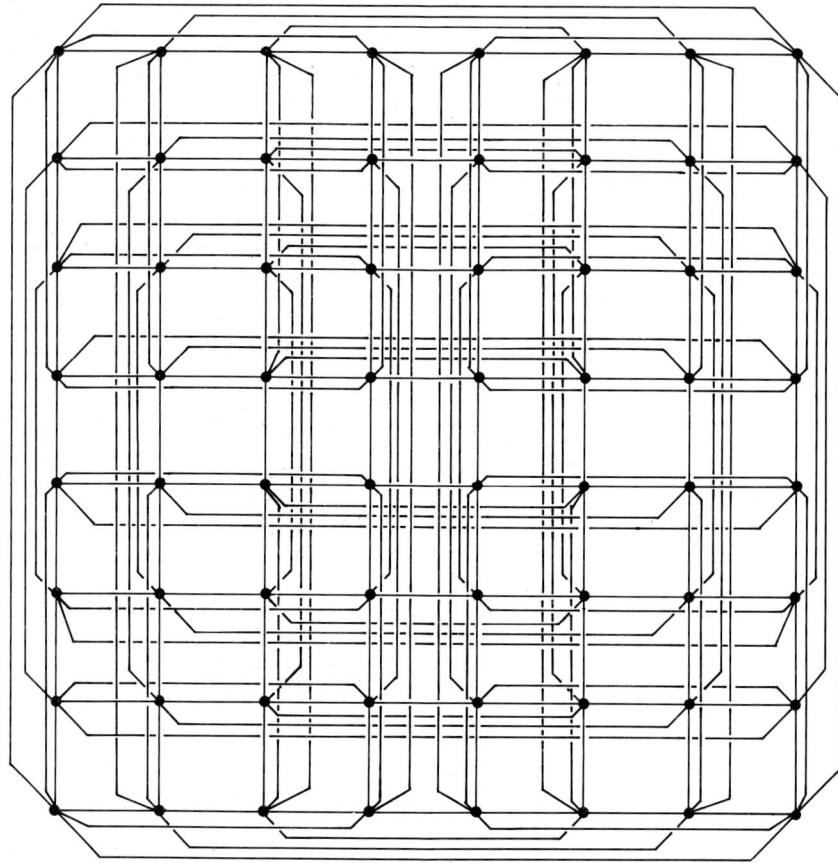

Fig. 4.11 Two-dimensional projection of six-dimensional hypercube showing connection paths between 64 processors.

which use messages to provide communication between processes, so that this is not a particularly novel development. In order to control the message-passing a kernel of the Cosmic Cube operating system is resident in each node in the hypercube. This allows a multiprocess environment to exist at each node with a number of virtual processes running on one processor. These kernels are responsible for creating and killing processes, scheduling their execution, managing the storage and dealing with error conditions. There is also a debug facility which allows the kernel to 'spy' on processes. The message routing and queueing mechanisms are also controlled currently by the kernel, both for communication between processes within a node and for messages which are routed through a node to and/or from other nodes. Eventually it is anticipated that some (if not all) of these functions may be incorporated into hardware or firmware at each node.

One problem with all multiprocessor systems is how to start a system which is distributed around a number of processors, with no master control unit. In the Cosmic Cube design this is done by connecting one node to a host processor and then sending start-up packets around the network (see Fig. 4.12).

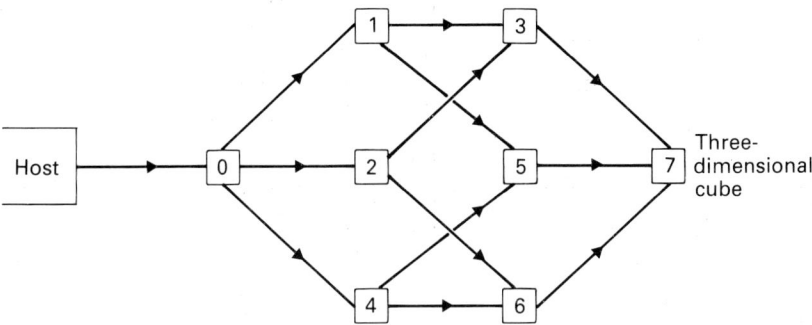

Fig. 4.12 Paths followed by start-up packets which check all communication paths from node 0 to node 7. Each node responds to the start-up message by returning messages report the failure back to node 0 and hence to the host.

The CalTech Cosmic Cube design represents a multiprocessor with nodes which are, in a sense, of arbitrary size. The designers are experimenting with nodes of differing sizes, and smaller or larger nodes may be more or less suitable for various applications. The current design is intended for compute-bound applications rather than i/o-bound applications. If i/o channels were connected to each node then possibly the design would be suitable for i/o-bound applications provided that we could utilize parallel i/o successfully (e.g. with real-time systems which have a number of sensors collecting data in parallel). The size of node in a multiprocessor is influenced by the relative speeds of interprocessor communication and processing. If communication between processors is slow we are clearly going to want to keep it to a minimum and probably have many processes running in a time-share fashion on a single processor. The current implementation has nodes running with a 5 MHz clock rate and utilizes channels which run at approximately 2 Mbps. Currently, applications programs run at a speed of up to 3 Mflops.

A building block for multiprocessors — the transputer

So far we have examined two designs which use multiple processing units. The first, the ICL DAP, used multiple ALUs rather than full CPUs. These ALUs were very simple indeed (only 1-bit processors), but nevertheless we can achieve significant parallel processing. The Cosmic Cube used off-the-shelf Intel 8086 processors and was a true MIMD design.

The INMOS group of companies have developed a single chip processor — the transputer, which they hope will be a useful building block for multiprocessors. It is designed specifically to be used in a multiprocessing environment by having built-in links which provide a serial message-passing facility at 10 Mbps as well as a peripheral interface. A block diagram of the 32-bit IMS T414 transputer is shown in Fig. 4.13. The transputer has been designed so that it can be connected in many different configurations, so a computer system can be configured easily to match an application area. In the first half of 1986, Floating Point Systems announced their T-series range of machines which use a hypercube interconnection method to produce a multiprocessor out of transputers. Nodes contain not only transputers but special purpose vector processors to improve performance on numerical problems. In order to be able to build a system with a

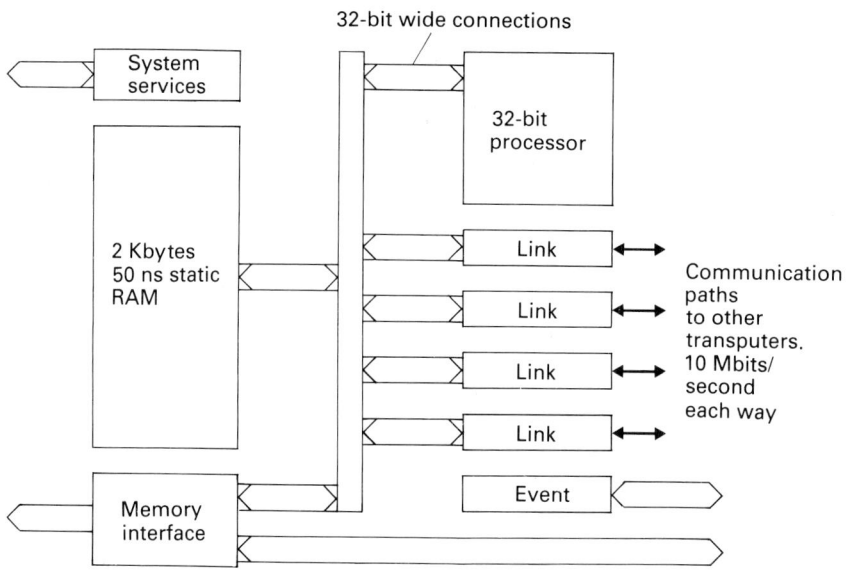

Fig. 4.13 Block diagram of transputer IMS T414.

reasonably large number of nodes the transputer links have been multiplexed to allow 16 connections to each transputer-based node. The top of the range T-series machine has 2048 nodes and a theoretical maximum speed of 262 Gflops.

The CalTech Cosmic Cube is programmed using conventional languages such as **C** or **Pascal,** with the addition of facilities to provide for the message-passing. Although transputers can be programmed in a similar way, INMOS has developed a special language (**occam**) based on the communicating sequential process model of concurrent computation. Occam processes can be either each resident on separate transputers or a number of them can reside upon a single transputer. The programmer can write in occam and remain ignorant of the number of transputers upon which his program will eventually run. It is even possible to write an occam program which can be run on a network of transputers which will determine the interconnection pattern automatically. We will be returning to the occam language when we discuss programming distributed and parallel processors in Part 3.

Summary

Having noted the levels at which parallel processing can occur we looked in this chapter at the various types of parallel architecture which exist. Firstly, we noted the broad classes of architecture suggested by Flynn. For parallel processing we are primarily interested in SIMD (single instruction, multidata) and MIMD (multi-instruction, multidata) machines, though we noted that pipelined machines might properly be included in SISD (single instruction, single data) machines. Flynn noted the different ways in which machines may be organized by classifying word-serial bit-parallel machines and word-parallel bit-serial machines (horizontal and vertical processing units). He also provided us with various sub-classes of array processors.

To round off the chapter we looked at the design of two types of parallel processor, the distributed array processor (e.g. the ICL DAP) and the true MIMD multiprocessor (e.g. the CalTech Cosmic Cube). We also looked at the transputer which has been proposed as a building block for future multiprocessors.

Further reading

The original classification schemes are given in Flynn (1966) and Shore (1973). Hockney & Jesshope (1981) present a readable summary of their approaches and develop a more detailed classification scheme of their own.

A fairly complete discussion of the design of the array processor is given by Parkinson in Evans (1982), and the Cosmic Cube design is described by Seitz (1985). For a description of the transputer the reader is referred to the current sales literature produced by INMOS or Whitby-Strevens (1985).

Part 2

Distributed Systems

So far in this book we have concentrated upon parallel processing systems. In the Introduction we pointed out that there was a close relationship between such systems and distributed processing systems. In this part we will discuss in more detail what is meant by a distributed processing system and also (in Chapter 7) discuss the design of a typical system.

Chapter 5

Fully Distributed Processing Systems

Three aspects of a computer system may be distributed — the hardware, the control and the database used. Figure 5.1 illustrates various stages in the decentralization of these three components of a system. The most centralized form of control is a single fixed central processor. Decentralization can be introduced by having master/slave processors or by replicating processors which are either totally autonomous or co-operating. The most

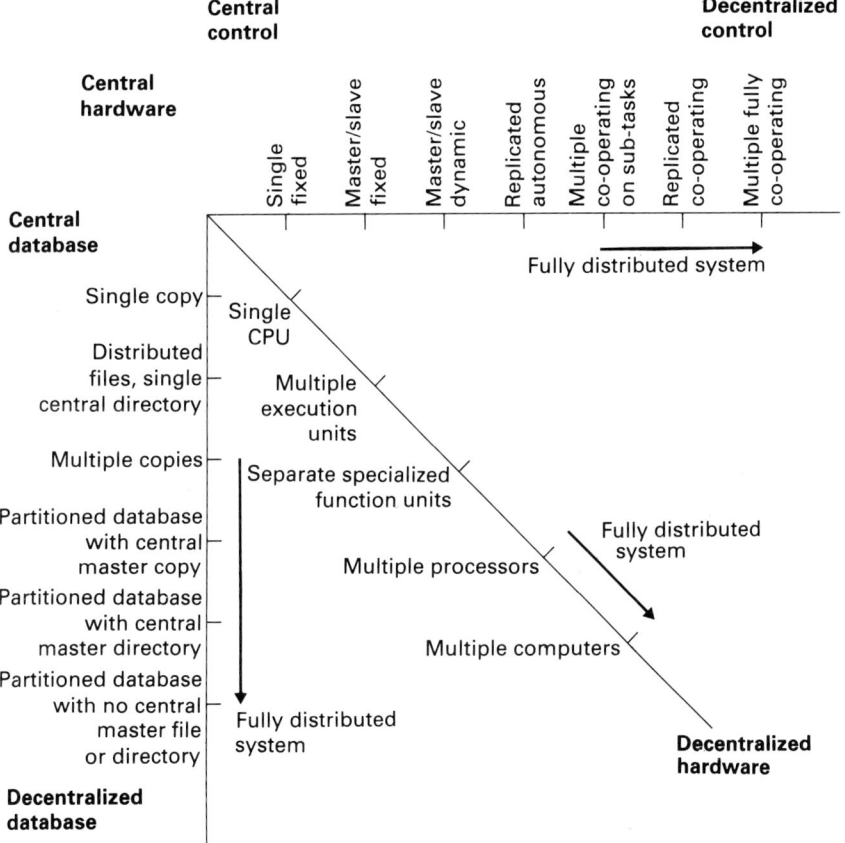

Fig. 5.1 Degrees of centralization in a data processing system showing possible definition of a fully distributed system.

distributed form of control arises with multiple fully co-operating processors.

In the above paragraph we have been considering logical processors. Decentralization of hardware is often considered to be of equal importance in the development of distributed systems and here we can have various options from a single central processing unit to multiple computers. The final aspect of decentralization is the database used by the system. A typical single processor system would have a single copy of the database on secondary storage. This can be distributed by having multiple copies of files and a single directory. The most decentralized form of database is one in which no single master copy or directory exists. It is possible to distinguish between systems in which data, control and hardware are only partially decentralized and those systems which may be termed **fully distributed systems,** which have a large degree of decentralization in all aspects. One possible definition of fully distributed systems is illustrated in Fig. 5.1.

In the following discussion of distributed processing systems it is important to realize that a distributed processing system represents a whole design philosophy. It is not just one criterion which can be used in the design of a processing system. This point will become clearer in a later chapter when we discuss some of the decisions which need to be made in the design of a distributed data processing system.

A key characteristic of a fully distributed system is the autonomy of its components. This implies that the components of the system can act independently; they can refuse requests made by other components; there is no such thing as a master/slave relationship between components. This leads to the possibility of components competing for work or resources.

By referring to components of a system we intend to include both logical and physical components. Whilst discussing the characteristics of the components of a distributed processing system we ought to consider the attractive concept of multiple components which can be allocated on a dynamic basis. Although a system which consists of a number of components each dedicated to a particular task might be considered (quite rightly) to be a distributed processing system, a system in which there are multiple components, each able to perform the same task, is a much more powerful concept.

These components of a distributed processing system must be able to communicate in some way. In a fully distributed processing system we would normally consider them to be connected by some sort of network. This implies that both parties to a communication have to accept some responsibility for controlling the interconnection; there exists some sort of two-party transfer protocol. The characteristics of the communication method can be discussed under two headings — logical and physical characteristics.

Logically we need some form of addressing mechanism. Ideally this should be such that the physical nature of the network is transparent to the communicating components. Transfer should be possible by referring to the logical name of the destination component and not the physical address.

The physical connection between components is often referred to as **coupling. Tight** coupling is done typically by the two parties to a communication sharing some form of executable memory by direct addressing. This is usually too close a linking method to be regarded as a network. Transfer of information is usually achieved by some form of master/slave protocol (e.g. register transfer). For a fully distributed processing system we normally require what is termed **loose** coupling, whereby information is transferred in the same way as input and output are normally performed. Such transfers are usually two-party co-operative transfers.

The characteristic difference between these two approaches is that the tighter the coupling, usually the faster the rate of transfer of information; that is the bandwidth is higher.

Users' view of distributed systems

Before moving on to look at some systems and asking whether they are examples of distributed processing systems, let us see briefly what a distributed processing system should look like to the user.

Ideally the user should not see a distributed processing system at all. He/she should see a unified system which provides a number of services and resources. The fact that one service (a certain compiler, say) is available on a certain processor in the distributed system and the user's files are stored elsewhere should be totally irrelevant to him/her.

In reality this ideal will not be achieved and the user will be aware that he/she is using a distributed system. The nearest to the ideal which is likely to be achieved is that the user is aware of some form of network operating system to control and supervise the allocation of resources. The next level of deterioration from the ideal is that the user becomes aware of the fact that there are multiple servers and has to refer to them specifically rather than just requesting services.

So far we have assumed that the user has been able to communicate with the network operating system and the servers in a common language. It may be necessary for the user to use a different language for different servers. The user will see this as having to use different languages when using different services. The next step down from the ideal is when the user becomes aware of having to select servers to select different services.

If the system is even farther from the ideal the user may become aware of what tasks are active on what servers, and have to consider how to balance the load between servers. Finally, at the lowest level of the distributed system the user becomes aware of the topology of the interconnection system between the servers and has to use this knowledge to control the servers and the communication between them.

Candidates for distributed processing systems

In this section we are going to present briefly three possible systems and pose the question — are they distributed processing systems?

In general we can say that a distributed processing system should have four characteristics. It should: (1) Have multiple processing units. (2) Provide some level of single system image. (3) Be connected electronically, and (4) Involve significant interaction between units.

The first example we will consider is that of a remote interconnected processing system. Typically a smaller college or university computer centre will maintain one or more medium size computers and have a link to a regional computer centre where larger jobs can be run on more powerful machines (see Fig. 5.2). Is this a distributed processing system?

Clearly there are multiple processing units (at least two). They may or may not provide some form of single image, depending upon the methods by which jobs can be submitted to the remote site. Normally this would at least require the user to be aware that he was submitting a remote job and would probably require him to know the JCL for the remote site.

The systems are connected electronically (by telephone line possibly), but the amount of interaction seems to be rather limited in most cases.

Clearly we could describe this system as a distributed processing system. In no way could we consider it to be a fully distributed system and in many ways it could be argued that the amount of interaction between the processors is so minimal that it does not merit being considered a distributed processing system.

The next candidate for a distributed processing system is the intelligent

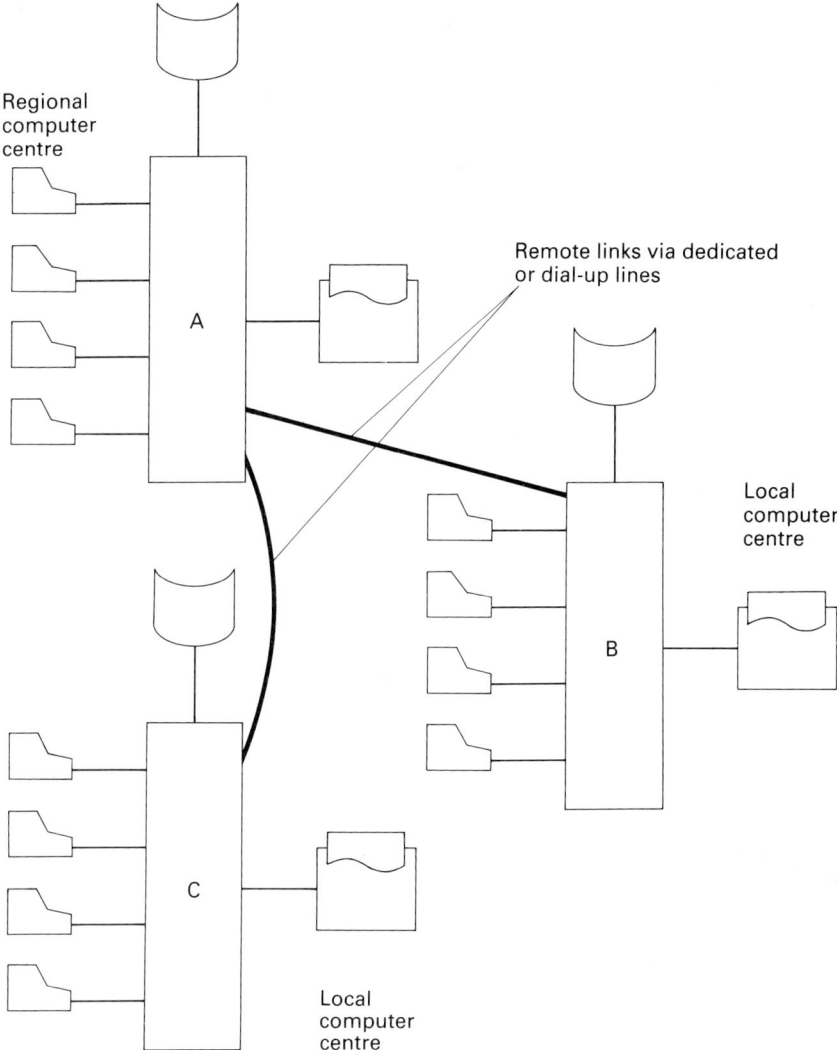

Fig. 5.2 Typical organization of computer centres linked to a regional centre.

peripheral type of system, illustrated in Fig. 5.3. There is an implied assumption in the definition of a distributed processing system that the PEs do some significant amount of processing. It is this ciriterion which would lead to one not considering an intelligent peripheral system as a distributed processing system. The difference in size of the two processing components is another potential criticism. Once again the answer is that although some

Chapter 5

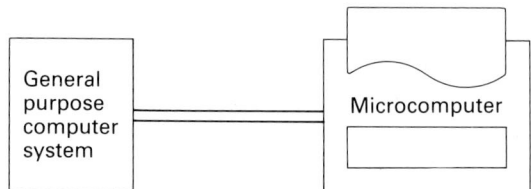

Fig. 5.3 Microcomputer being used as an intelligent terminal to a central computer system.

processing is distributed, such a system would probably not be considered to be a distributed processing system.

Our final example is a multiprocessor, illustrated in Fig. 5.4. Is this a distributed processing system? Firstly let us list the arguments for it being considered to be one

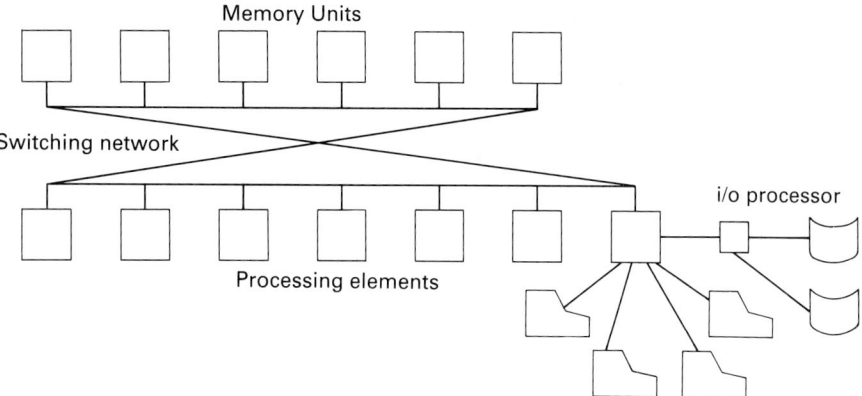

Fig. 5.4 Possible shared memory multiprocessor architecture.

(1) We have multiple processing units, each carrying out some significant processing, and they are all of comparable size.
(2) The system certainly presents a single systems image — the user believes he is using a single processor.
(3) The processors are interconnected electronically.
(4) There is a significant amount of interaction between the processors.

Now for some of the arguments against considering a multiprocessor as a distributed processing system.
(1) The processing units are not 'complete' in some sense, as each unit is not an independent node. Therefore it does not demonstrate the

Fully Distributed Processing Systems

characteristics of reliability and availability one would expect in a distributed processing system. Against this we must accept that some degree of fault tolerance is possible since each processor is capable of duplicating some of the work of others which fail.

(2) The configuration is possible only if the processors are physically close. It is often assumed that a distributed processing system must involve distributing processing physically over some distance. This is not necessarily the case. Really, we only require logical distribution.

The above arguments suggest that a multiprocessor is a distributed processing system. In many ways it is, but it is often more convenient to consider it as a parallel processor as it has many of the characteristics of such systems. It is the close relationship between these two concepts which is the basis for this book.

None of the above systems characterizes neatly what we might consider to be a distributed processing system. The existence of multiple processing units is not sufficient to make a system a distributed processing system. Let us now pose the opposite question: are they necessary?

Consider the possibility of a number of users using a large single processor machine. They are each running a virtual machine. It is logically possible to envisage writing systems which use these virtual machines to co-operate on some task. Isn't this logically a distributed processing system? Clearly the concept of a distributed processing system is a logical one, which can be mapped on to either a number of virtual machines running on one single processor or a number of independent machines.

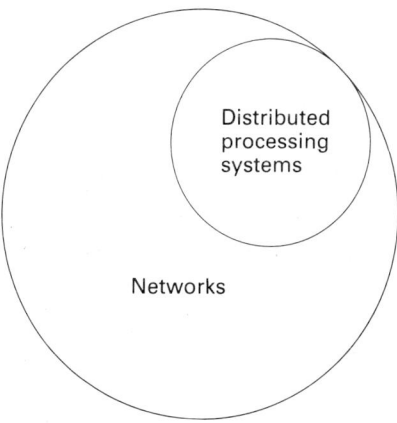

Fig. 5.5 Relationship between networks and distributed processing systems.

Indeed, anywhere in between these two extremes is possible. Thus we must consider distributed processing to be a logical design concept which can be mapped on to the physical concept of a distributed computer system.

Networks are means of connecting numbers of computers together. A distributed processing system is one in which a number of processors have some sort of interaction to perform a task; this interaction being at a higher (and looser) level than that required for a parallel processor.

There are infinite possible levels of interaction between a simple network used only for file transfer, which we would not consider to be a distributed processing system, and tightly connected systems which we would consider to be multiprocessor computers. Distributed computing systems come somewhere in between. This concept is illustrated in Fig. 5.5.

In Chapter 7 we will consider how a true distributed processing system could be designed to run on a distributed computer system. In the next chapter we will consider in more detail the ways in which processors can be connected to form distributed processing systems.

Summary

In this chapter we have discussed the nature of distributed processing systems and shown how they are a logical concept which may or may not be mapped on to a physically distributed computer system. We have not succeeded in producing a clear definition of distributed processing, but we have defined a fully distributed processing system (that is one extreme of a distributed processing system) and illustrated by example the interface between the other extreme and parallel processors. This border is less well defined and in some ways illustrated the need for a text such as this which covers both distributed parallel processing.

Further reading

The definition of a fully distributed processing system is based on Enslow's work at Georgia Tech. This is reported in his contribution to the Loughborough Crest course on Parallel Processing Systems (Evans, 1982). Chapter 1 of Lorin (1980) also provides a good overview of the nature of distributed processing systems.

Chapter 6

Networks and Interconnection Structures

Having given a general indication of the nature of distributed computing systems (including both logical and physical distribution), we now want to look at how the logical distribution of processing can be mapped on to computing systems at various levels. Figure 6.1 illustrates the various levels which exist in a computer system. The various levels of distribution are shown in Fig. 6.2.

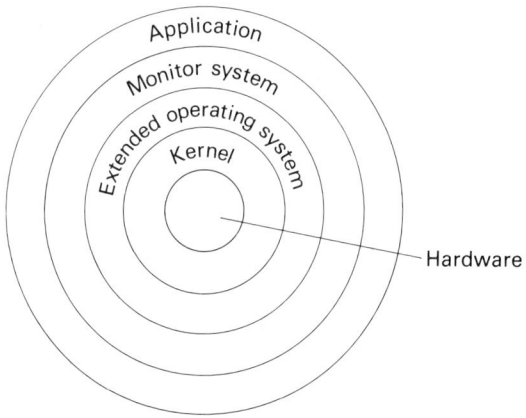

Fig. 6.1 System levels.

Figure 6.2a shows distribution at the highest level, the application level. Figure 6.2b illustrates a system operating with different monitors sharing a common base operating system. It is possible for a system to run multiple operating systems. These would then have a shared kernel and the user would see a number of virtual machines (see Fig. 6.2c). The final step, Fig. 6.2d, is complete partitioning and the use of dedicated hardware. An alternative way of looking at this is shown in Fig. 6.3.

Distribution is the result of a system design process. The stages in this process can be listed as below
(1) Define partitions of work (by application or function or geography).
(2) Define partitions of data (by similar criteria).

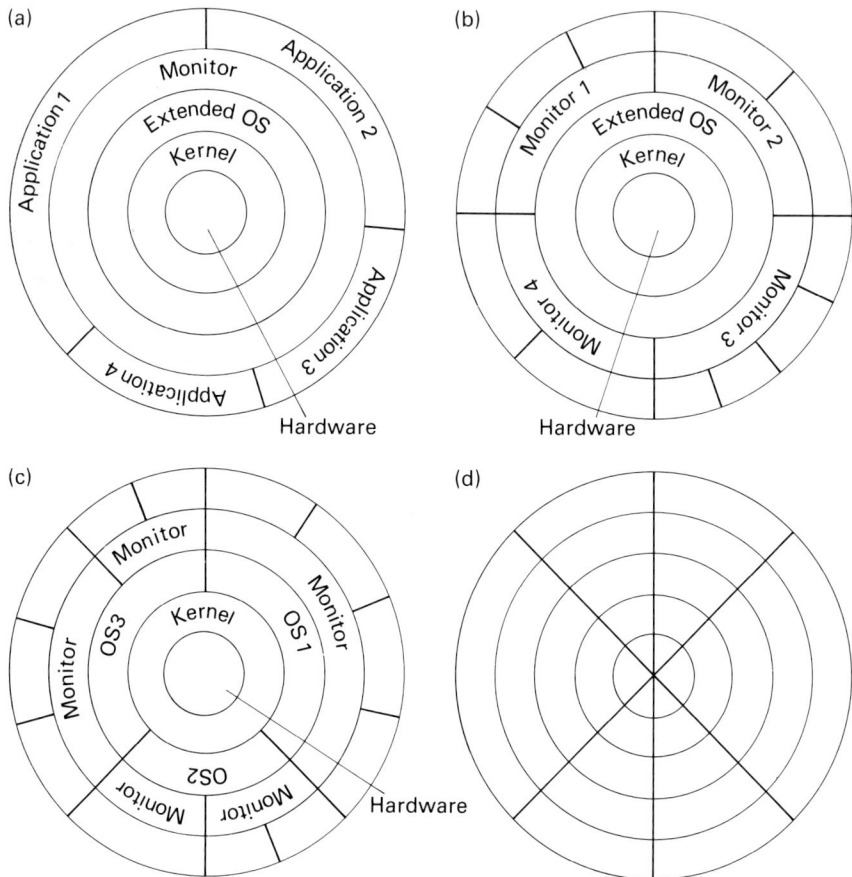

Fig. 6.2 Levels of distribution. (a) Node with shared applications; (b) Multiple sub-systems with shared operating system; (c) Virtual machines; (d) Complete partitioning with dedicated hardware.

(3) Identify relationships between data and work.
(4) Recognize relationships between partitions.
(5) Determine a possible set of work structures.
(6) Define a set of potential hardware bases.
(7) Choose hardware.

Let us now examine briefly the last of these, the selection of hardware. The next chapter will look at the earlier stages by considering a simple example. Assuming that we have decided that we need a distributed computer system, we need to know how we can connect the individual processors together.

Networks and Interconnection Structures 65

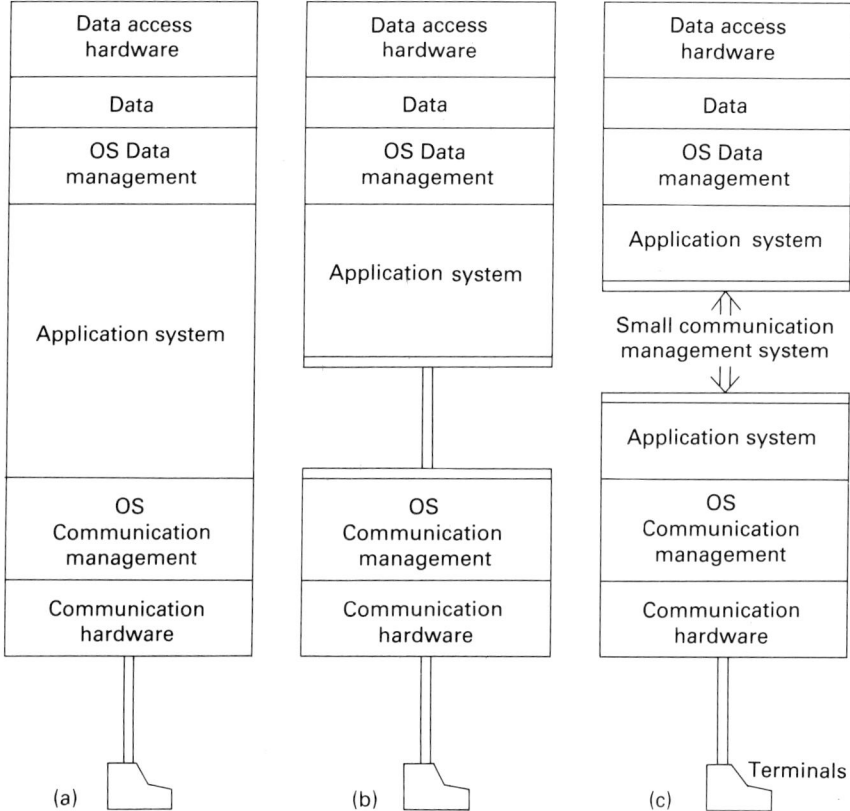

Fig. 6.3 Degrees of distribution possible with a single application. (a) Non distributed; (b) Distributed function; (c) Distributed processing.

The three basic system structures available to us are hierarchic, peer and compound (see Fig. 6.4). Figure 6.5 illustrates a typical decomposed functional hierarchy and Fig. 6.6 shows another hierarchical system which has been partitioned according to application.

We still have a number of alternative interconnection methods. These can be split into two categories, those with a single connection system (pipe, ring or hopping — see Fig. 6.7) and those with multiple connection paths (e.g. multiple bus, star or mesh — see Fig. 6.8).

The final alternative is whether or not the same connection method is used throughout the system. Figure 6.9 shows two peer systems; one with a homogeneous connection method (multiple bus) and one with a heterogeneous connection system using a central control processor.

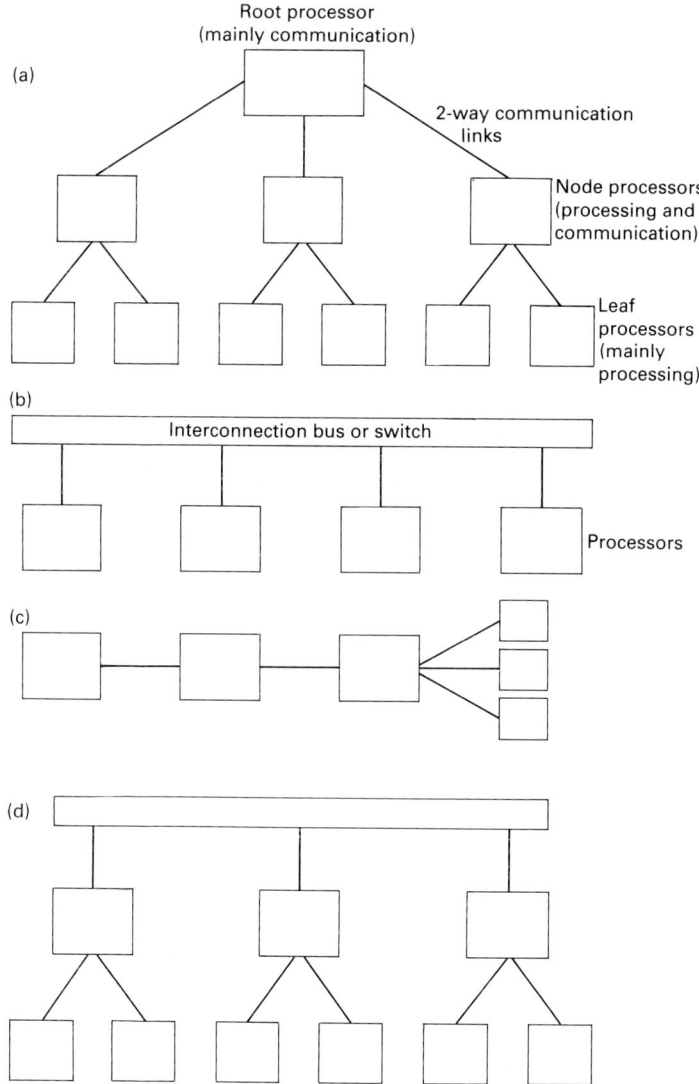

Fig. 6.4 Possible interconnection structures. (a) Hierarchic interconnection structure; (b) Peer interconnection structure; (c) Three peer processors (one with sub-hierarchy); (d) Three peer processors (each with hierarchy).

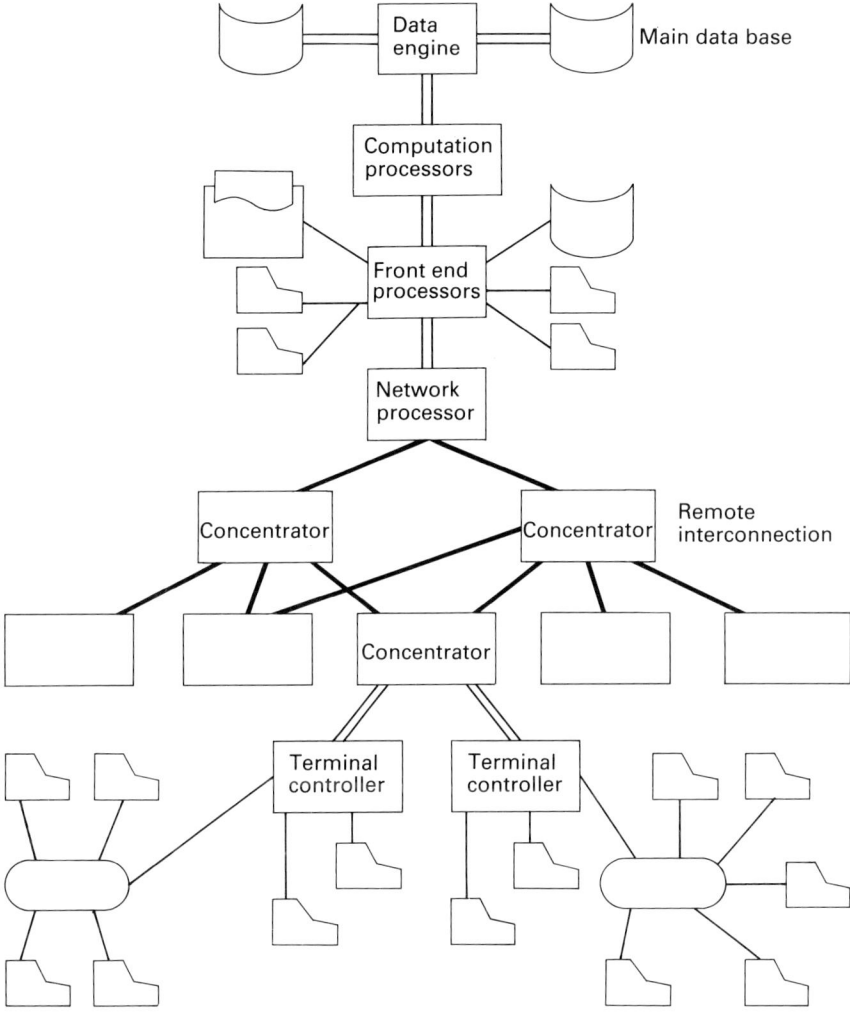

Fig. 6.5 Typical decomposed functional hierarchy.

All the above systems might be considered to be forms of networks. A network is essentially any system of providing communication between two or more computers. Networks can be split into two categories according to their application — wide area networks (WANs) which by definition cover large physical areas (up to the size of countries, continents or even the world) and local area networks (LANs) which are typically used by a single organization on a single site. The dividing line between these two

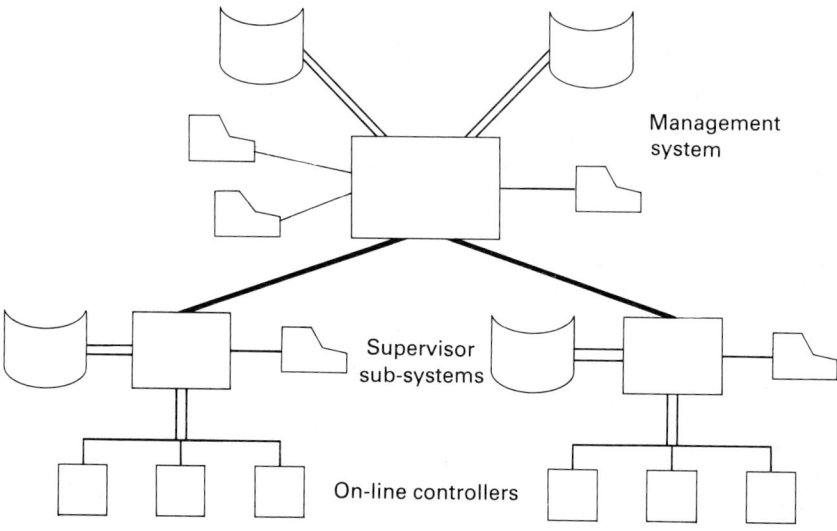

Fig. 6.6 Hierarchical system decomposed according to application.

categories may clearly be difficult to draw, but many of the fundamental ideas are common to both.

In an ideal world all the computers or components of a distributed system would be in direct communication with each other. The implementor would then be left with deciding only on an encoding scheme and whether to use asynchronous or synchronous transmission. Asynchronous transmission involves an overhead in that it requires an initial start-bit to be sent (usually before each character) in order to notify the receiver when a character is to be sent. It has the advantage over synchronous transmission, however, of usually being easier and cheaper to implement. Synchronous transmission requires a link between the clocks of the sender and receiver. This can be provided either by a separate clock line or by encoding the clock signal within the transmitted data.

Various encoding schemes are possible. Their aim is to send as much information as possible in the least number of bits whilst still providing some error checking capability. There is clearly going to be some trade-off between these two requirements, as any error checking information is redundant (excess) information, in the sense that it does not convey any additional information. The cost of transmission is likely to rise the greater the distance. Increasing cost suggests a need for both an economical transmission system and and a reliable one. The simplest form of error

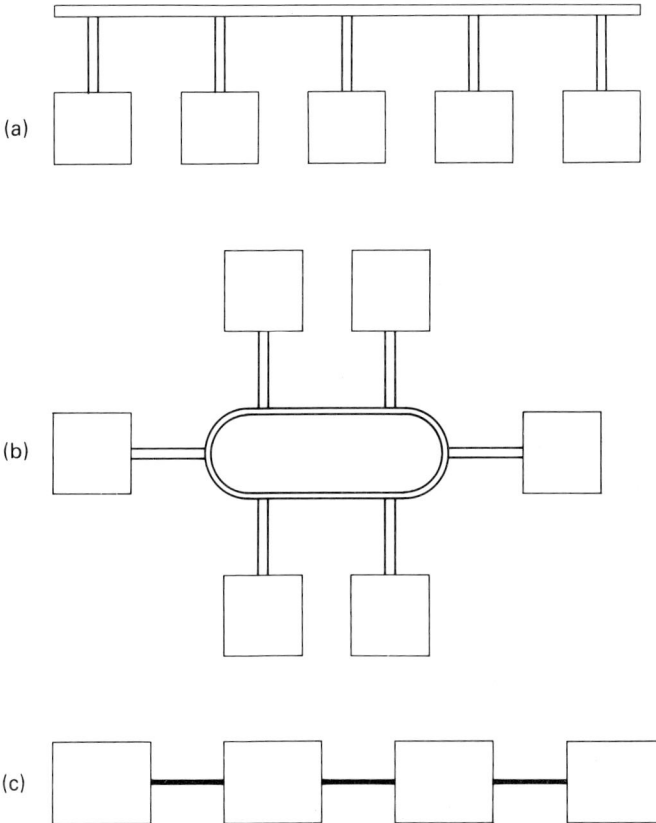

Fig. 6.7 Single connection path systems. (a) Comm bus or pipe connection; (b) Ring connection; (c) 'Hopping' — communication between non-neighbours involves intermediate processors.

checking is the standard parity checking method, but this can only detect errors in one bit. The encoding mechanisms which can be used depend upon the size of the set of information which is going to be transmitted.

These considerations also apply in practical networks when not all possible physical connections between components of the system exist. Here though, we have the added complication of some form of switching system. This mechanism can affect our choice of coding and transmission system. Three switching techniques in common use are circuit switching, message switching and packet switching. We will now consider briefly each of these in turn.

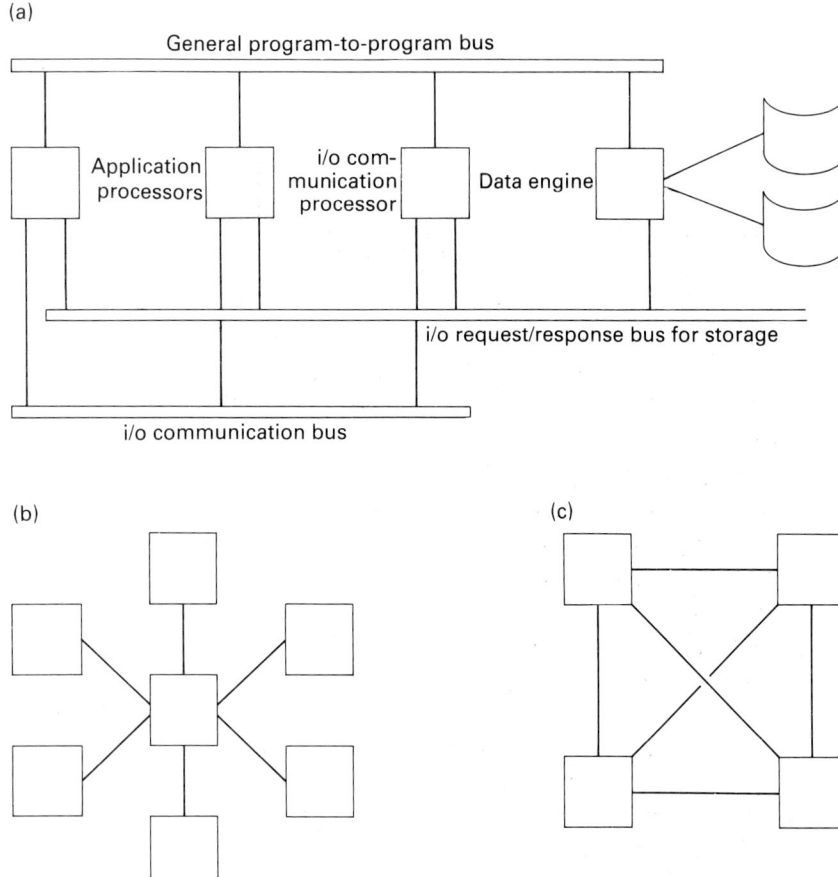

Fig. 6.8 Multiple connection path systems. (a) Multiple bus connection; (b) Star connection pattern; (c) Mesh connection pattern.

Circuit switching

Communication consists of three phases with circuit switching. The first phase involves the establishment of a dedicated communication path through the network between the two parties to the communication. In a star network this only involves the central node of the star, which is probably dedicated to this task anyway. With uniform ring structures some way of deciding which way round the ring the communication path is to be established is required. One factor to be considered is whether each communication link within the network is capable of carrying one or

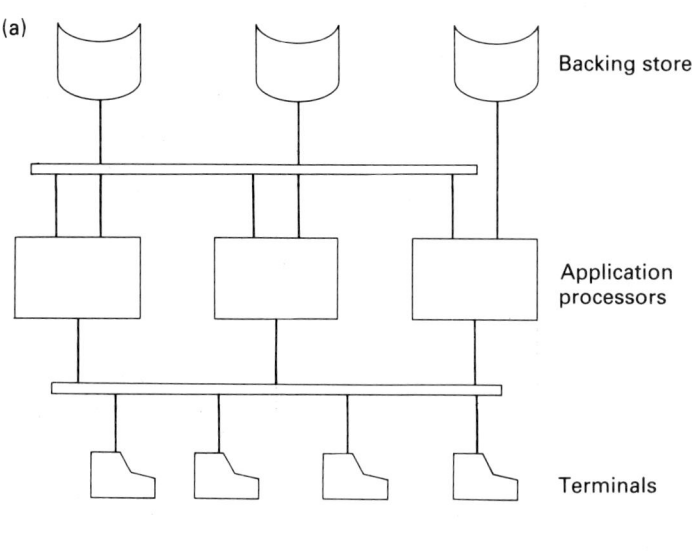

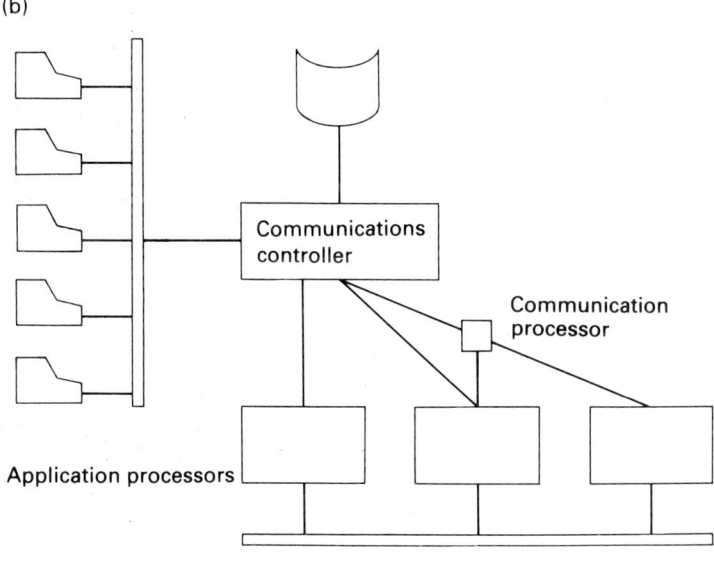

Fig. 6.9 Two different peer interconnection systems. (a) Peer homogeneous system (multiple bus); (b) Peer heterogeneous system with central control processor.

multiple sets of transmission. If only one transmission is allowed per link then in some topologies the establishment of a communication path can effectively prevent some nodes from communicating with any other part of the network for the duration of the transmission. Providing multiple transmission paths along a link will almost certainly increase the cost.

Having established the link the next phase is to actually perform the data transfer. This can now be carried out as though a permanent link existed. The final phase of the communication is to release the link.

Both the first and last phases are complicated by the fact that, in most networks, any node on the network is allowed to request communication. We can therefore get two nodes requesting incompatible communication paths.

The main disadvantage of circuit switching is that channel capacity is dedicated to a particular communication, even if no data is currently being transferred. The main advantage is that once the connection is established (which can take an appreciable time) the network becomes transparent to the users and communication can take place at a rapid rate, making fully interactive communication possible.

For WANs, circuit switching is usually appropriate only if the load is light and/or intermittent, when dial-up lines can be used, or if the load is very heavy and sustained, when leased dedicated lines can prove cost-effective.

Message switching

Instead of establishing a dedicated link, with the message switching approach a node merely prepends an address (destination node) on to any message and sends it to its nearest or least busy neighbour. If the node has more than one such neighbour it may determine which to send the message to by having a database indicating which neighbour lies on the shortest path to the destination of the message. Of course it is possible that the sending node is not actually aware of the topology of the network, or exactly where the destination node is. When a node receives a message which is not addressed to it, it forwards the message on, hopefully in the direction of the ultimate destination. Clearly some way is required to prevent messages being sent endlessly around a network and failing to be sent on to the ultimate destination. Having received a message, a node can send an acknowledgement message which has to find its path back through the network.

Message switching has a number of advantages over circuit switching.

Networks and Interconnection Structures

Line utilization is higher because we do not have dedicated lines lying idle whilst no data transfer is taking place. Therefore less total transmission capacity is needed.

Circuit switching requires both sender and receiver to be available for data transfer. In message switching messages can be held if the receiver is not ready. Furthermore, messages can be sent to multiple receivers. Because there is no dedicated line, no communication path can be blocked as can happen with circuit switching. Furthermore, message priorities are easier to establish.

Essentially in message switching the nodes take a more active part in the communication process. This makes error checking and coding translation (for example from ASCII to EBCDIC) easier to incorporate, but the users pay for this by the fact that messages generally take longer to pass through the network. A message switched system is not suitable for interactive communication.

Packet switching

With message switching the length of the message sent by a node is determined by that node. Packet switching restricts the length of the messages which can be sent (a typical maximum is a few thousand bits). These part-messages are termed packets. One immediate advantage of this approach over message switching is that because of the predictability of the size of messages it is easier for nodes to retain a copy of a message (or packet) just sent to aid in error recovery.

By splitting a message into sections we can instantly obtain faster transmission. Once the first part of the message has been transferred along the first part of the route through the network and is on its way on the second part, transmission of the second packet can commence. We can thus overlap the transmission of messages in a way which is analogous to the way in which a pipeline processor can speed up the processing of instructions.

We will now look in more detail at two ways in which whole messages can be split into packets and transmitted over the network.

The first approach we will consider is the **datagram** approach. A message which is longer than one packet is split into a number of packets, each with their own destination address. These packets (or datagrams — from data telegrams?) are then treated independently. This can mean that each part of the message may be sent via a different route through the network depending on how busy each node is. Once a packet has been sent to a particular node, that node is not immediately available to receive the next packet so it is quite likely that the next datagram will be sent to a different node. We therefore have the possibility of parallel processing of the communication which has clear implications for the speed of transmission. One drawback, however, is that datagrams may arrive at their destination in the wrong order, so we require extra intelligence at the receiver in order to sort them out.

An alternative to the datagram approach is the **virtual circuit** approach. This method is closer to the circuit switching method we discussed earlier, and thus gains some of the advantages of the speed of circuit switching. Prior to the transmission of packets, a logical connection path is established between sender and receiver. Note that the logical connection does not imply a dedicated path. Part or all of the connection path can be shared by many logical routes unlike the circuit switching method. Each packet now carries a virtual circuit identifier. Because each node now has less work to do in deciding where to send the packet, the delay at each node is reduced. The price paid for this is the cost of establishing the logical connection.

Both approaches to packet switching can provide transmission speeds which are adequate for interactive communication. The datagram approach is usually considered more appropriate for shorter messages where the cost of setting up the logical connection is relatively high. Packet switching usually achieves the highest line utilization level of all three approaches. One way of making packet switched networks cost-effective for WANs is to provide a public connection utility such as the PSS network run by British Telecom in the UK, and the TELENET and TYMNET services in the United States.

Local networks

So far we have not considered what effect the size of the network has upon the communication protocols used. We will now consider local networks and see what effect the (relatively) small size of these networks has. Because of the limited physical separation between nodes in an LAN it is often the case that a simple network topology is used. For example, a simple ring or bus connection method is common. One consequence of this is that there is only a single transmission path linking all nodes. It is therefore necessary to ensure fair use of this medium. We will outline briefly three possible ways in which this can be achieved for bus and ring structures.

(1) The **Carrier-Sense-Multiple-Access with Collision Detection (CSMA/CD)** method is suitable for use with bus networks. All the nodes are connected directly to the same cable which therefore operates in a **multiple access** mode. Any information which is to be sent over the network is first packaged by the sending node into a **frame** with the destination address included at the head of the frame. This frame is then broadcast over the network and can be detected by all nodes. The node whose address is in the frame reads the whole frame, not just the address, and can respond according to a specified protocol. The address of the sending node is also included in the header of each frame so that a responding node knows where to send any response.

If two or more frames were transmitted simultaneously then clearly the data would be corrupted. In an effort to reduce this possibility, any node which wishes to transmit a frame listens to the network first to detect if any frame is currently being transmitted. This can be done by merely sensing the presence of a carrier signal. Transmission is then deferred until after the transmission of that frame is complete.

It is still possible, however, for two (or more) nodes to await the end of the transmission of a frame and then start transmitting their own frames simultaneously. A **collision** is then said to have occurred. To detect this the sending node monitors the network and if the transmitted and received signals differ it assumes that a collision has occurred. Having detected a collision, it ensures that all other nodes detect the collision by sending a random bit pattern known as a **jamming sequence.** Retransmission is tried after a random delay. Provided that the load on the network is not too great then there is a high probability that this method will allow all necessary frames to be sent. With LANs the transmission rate over a network can be high (up to about 10 Mbps), so loadings tend to be low, allowing this approach to be feasible.

(2) The use of a **control** or **permission token** is an alternative approach which can be used with both bus and ring networks. Before transmitting any information a node must be in possession of a control token. This token is passed from one node to another according to a set of rules understood by all nodes. The following sequence of operations is performed.

(a) A logical ring is established linking all the nodes in the network and a single control token created.

(b) The token is passed from node to node around the logical ring until it is received by a node which wishes to transmit a frame (or frames) of information.

76   *Chapter 6*

(c) This node can then send its frames, and then pass on the control token to the next node on the logical ring.

Assuming that no node needs to retain the control token for an excessive length of time this method can work perfectly satisfactorily. This requirement is equivalent to the need for a relatively low load on the network as a low load implies a low message transmission rate.

(3) The final method we will consider is suitable only for ring networks. In this method a **slotted ring** is established. This means that the ring is first established to contain a fixed number of bits by a special node on the ring called a **monitor**.

As each bit is received by a node it is examined by the node then passed on to the next node. The monitor ensures that the number of bits circulating in the ring remains constant. The complete ring is arranged to contain a fixed number of slots, each of which contains a fixed number of bits capable of carrying a fixed-size frame of information. This frame contains control bits (which indicate whether the packet or slot is full or empty) as well as the destination and source address and the data. Initially, all frames are empty. When a node wishes to transmit a frame of information, it waits until it receives an empty slot and then proceeds to fill it with the desired information. Each slot also contains response bits which are updated by receiving nodes, so that a transmitting node can detect if its message has been received. It is the responsibility of the transmitting node to release the slot and mark it empty. To ensure a fair distribution of access to the network, each node is usually limited to being able to transmit only one frame of information at once.

The main disadvantage of the slotted ring approach is the reliance it places on a special monitor node to maintain the slotted ring structure.

Summary

We have considered the various levels at which distribution can occur, and we indicated briefly some of the interconnection structures which can be used. The rest of the chapter discussed the logical ways in which data can be transmitted over such networks. What we have not discussed is the actual physical media over which data can be transmitted. These can include multicore cables (possibly allowing for parallel transmission), coaxial cables (which are essentially serial devices) and, more recently, fibre optic cables. Other options for longer distances can include microwave transmission or broadcast radio transmission. The main difference to be noted with radio communication is that the same message is transmitted simultaneously to a number of receivers; thus an all node to all node interconnection structure is much easier to visualize. A major problem can be interference in the transmissions. Further discussion of this topic is best left to electrical engineering texts.

Further reading

A number of text books have been written on the subject of data communication and computer networks. Many of them, however, are aimed at the Electrical Engineer rather than the Computer Scientist. Halsall (1985) is aimed at both groups of students and is an appropriate next step for the interested reader. If your interest is more in LANs then Stallings (1984) provides an excellent discussion of this field after introducing the general concepts of networks. For an introduction to networks with particular reference to their use with microcomputers the recent book by Jesty (1985) is recommended.

Chapter 7

Designing a Distributed Processing System

There are two basic approaches to designing a distributed computing system. These are the **top-down** approach and the **bottom-up** approach.

The bottom-up approach is exemplified by systems which are built from existing separate systems. Typically, an organization would have a number of independent systems operating in a number of different departments or offices. It is decided that some form of connection between these systems is required. One solution is to off-load the non-urgent batch processing jobs on to a larger central machine. Updating company-wide records would be a typical batch job suitable for processing on a central machine. Such a design is illustrated in Fig. 7.1. We may talk about such a system as being **co-operative computing,** rather than true distributed computing.

A similar system might result from a decision to off-load some interactive work from an overloaded central facility. Small interactive systems would be purchased for use in individual departments and offices. The difference between this sort of system and a true top-down designed distributed computing system is that the system behaves as a number of co-operating, but independent, parts rather than as a unified system. To achieve a unified system image the system must be designed as a whole, and this implies a form of top-down design.

As an example, consider the position of an organization whose present single processor system is in need of replacement. By assessing the future needs for the system it becomes apparent that it is extremely unlikely that any single processor will be capable of providing an adequate service in the future. The need for a system which is highly reliable, always available, quickly installed, cost-effective, capable of giving a predictable response and able to grow with minimum disruption suggests that a distributed processing system is required.

A distributed processing system will give high reliability because the failure of one component need not imply total system failure and we have the possibility of duplication of essential functions. Similar arguments apply to the need for high availability. The requirement for a predictable response suggests that response to the user should ideally be separated from the total use of the system and linked to a more local usage. Large systems tend to grind to a halt when a large number of users are connected.

Designing a Distributed Processing System

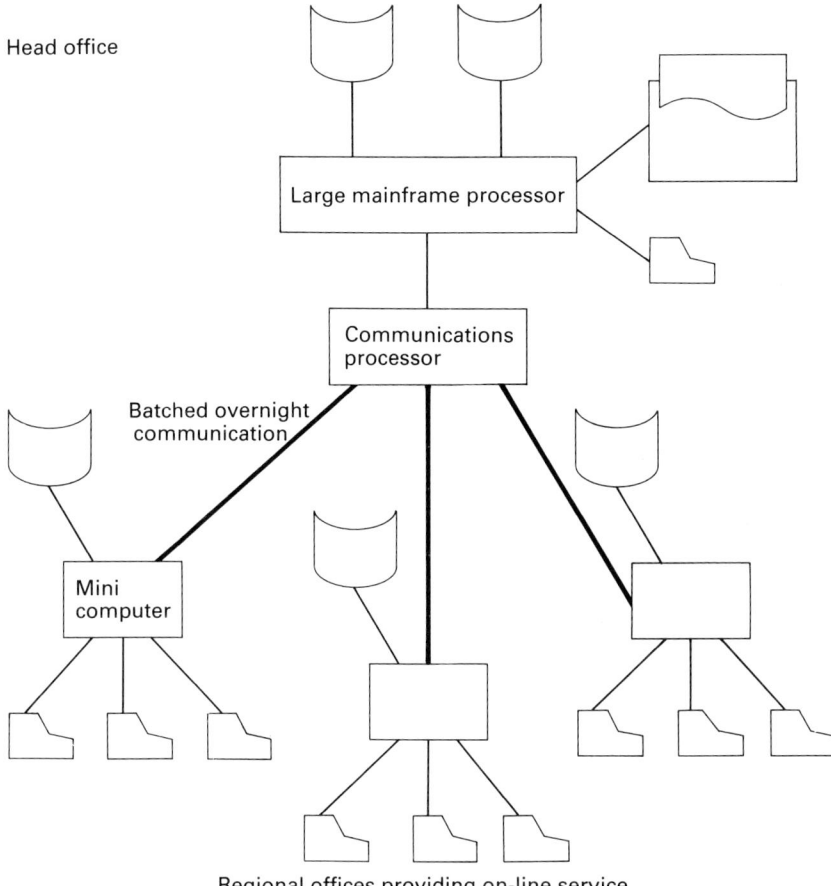

Fig. 7.1 Co-operative computing — building upon existing systems.

If the same users are spread out over a number of systems then the response should be more predictable.

A distributed computing system should be able to expand with a minimum of disruption for two reasons. Firstly, the system is designed to include a number of components so adding extra ones should be relatively straightforward. Secondly, only part of the system should be off-line whilst additional components are added, thus minimizing the disruption to users of the system as a whole.

That a distributed system would satisfy the requirements for quick installation and cost-effectiveness is less easy to justify. A few comments can be made though. A distributed system may be installed in stages, making the installation less disruptive and apparently quicker to individual users. The potential for expansion of a distributed system implies that there is less need to allow for extra capacity to begin with, reducing the initial cost.

The design of a distributed computer system requires decisions to be made on both the physical and logical distribution of processing. One possibility is based on a **peer locally interconnected system.** That is a system which consists of a number of equal powerful processing nodes cooperating (peer), but physically close to each other (not geographically dispersed). Having decided on such a physical distribution the next task is to decide on the logical distribution of tasks. One possibility is a partitioning of tasks by **application** or **responsibility.**

Assume that the company's activities could be divided into three reasonably separate areas of activity (e.g. sales, service and accounts). A distributed processing system could consist of three processors, one for each area of responsibility, as shown in Fig. 7.2.

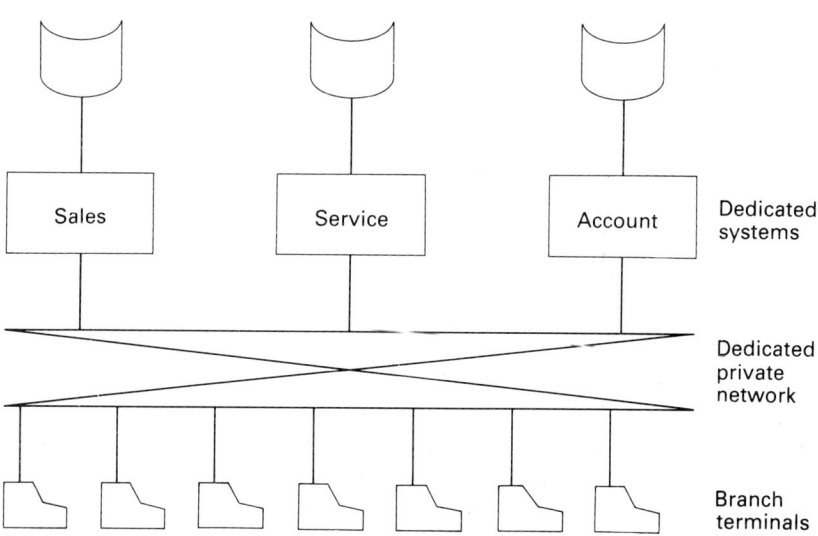

Fig. 7.2 Partitioned system. Each system deals with one particular area of responsibility or application.

Designing a Distributed Processing System

There are a number of potential problems with such a simplistic approach
(1) The workload in some (or all) of the application areas may still be too large for single processor systems to be satisfactory.
(2) The interconnection of terminals giving each terminal access to each sub-system is quite likely to be uneconomic even if it is physically possible.
(3) Although the management is such that the sales and accounts divisions are separate, it is quite possible that they would use a common database so that the physical distribution of the functions may be undesirable even though a logical distribution is attractive.

The problem of some of the distributed tasks being too large for single machines suggests that we need to consider alternative partitioning methods. One such approach is a **geographic partition.** Suppose that the company's activities were split between two regions (e.g. Scotland and England/Wales). It might now be sensible to partition the processing both by application and by region, as illustrated in Fig. 7.3. No link is shown between the two service departments as these could operate reasonably independently of each other.

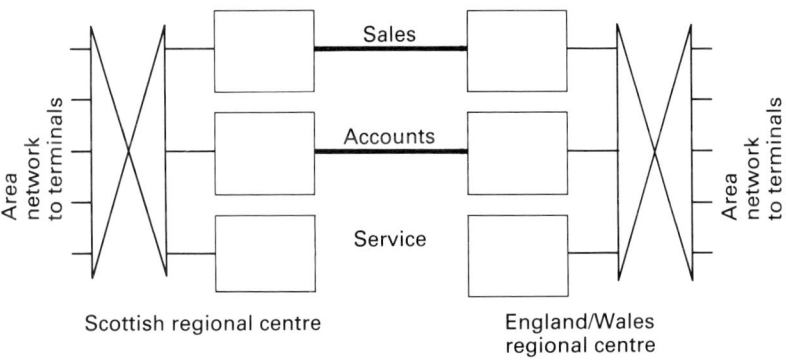

Fig. 7.3 System partitioned by application and geography.

Although we have shown all six machines to be installed at a central site, it would be equally possible to consider the two physically separate regional computer centres. The arguments against decentralization are that the functions carried out at the two regional centres are likely to be functionally similar and the installations at the sites are likely to be physically similar. There is a sense therefore in which design and management decisions relating to the two centres are carried out at a level above the two centres so that it makes sense to keep the data processing control centralized.

On the other hand, having two regional centres may reduce communication costs since presumably communication costs between the shops/offices would be less if they were only connected to a regional rather than a national centre. It is of course necessary to allow for the intercentre communication costs and set this off against the potential savings of two centres.

There are also a number of decisions to be taken about the type of communication which is required between the sites
(1) Should a private network be set up or should the services of a common carrier or specialized network supplier be used?
(2) Is it possible to envisage using the public telephone network for communication? If so, are dedicated lines required, or should we rely on dial-up?
(3) What sort of communication speed is required; should we use multiplexing?
(4) Is it necessary to maintain alternative routes in case one connection goes down?

The answers to all these questions depend upon the amount of communication required between the sites and how urgent that communication is.

This geographic partitioning may still not reduce the load on individual processors to a sufficiently low level that we can have confidence in the ability of uniprocessors to be able to provide an adequate service now and cope with future expansion. Furthermore, there are some possible reliability concerns to be considered.

Ideally the malfunction of one processor should not bring the system down. A stand-by processor should be available (this is particularly true if we consider something like a banking system rather than a retail system). In the event of a malfunction rendering part of the system inoperative the impact of this failure should be felt by as few customers as possible.

Response time at each shop/office should be predictable and stable.

A partial solution to these problems might be to divide the workload even further into smaller regions or even individual offices or shops. Now it may or may not be necessary to maintain the application partitioning we introduced to start with. One possible configuration is shown in Fig. 7.4.

The problem of predictable response is tackled by reducing the potential workload on each machine. This solution also minimizes the

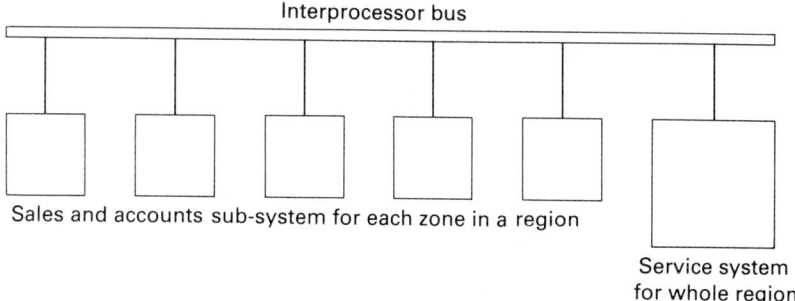

Fig. 7.4 Local geographic partitioning at a central site. Each processor would also be connected to a regional terminal network (possibly divided into two or three areas).

impact of failure to a smaller region and allows for the possibility of a single smaller standby unit which could be available to take over the processing of a single sub-region rather than having a standby processor available to take over the processing for a whole region. This assumes that the sub-region processors are tightly coupled and located at a regional centre rather than distributed amongst the sub-regions. The same arguments about decentralization apply again at this level, but the need for intercommunication between sub-regions is assumed to be higher than that between regions.

So far, each processor has carried out all the tasks associated with a particular application in a particular region or sub-region. An alternative approach to distributing the processing is to partition the tasks themselves so that each processor performs a different function. An example of such a **functional partitioning** is shown in Fig. 7.5. Here we have introduced the concept of a gateway processor which handles all the communications between remote terminals and the processing units. It can also handle the communication between regions. This opens the door to increased flexibility in the allocation of tasks to sub-region processes. Also, the boundaries of sub-regions can be changed easily and new sub-regions created if more processors are available without expensive reconnection of terminals to sub-region processors.

The gateway processor could be responsible for performing some of the simpler interactions with remote terminals without referring back to the main processing unit. For example, it could have access to a price database and transactions could be referred to sales only when actual purchases were made. We should also consider the possibility of extending this

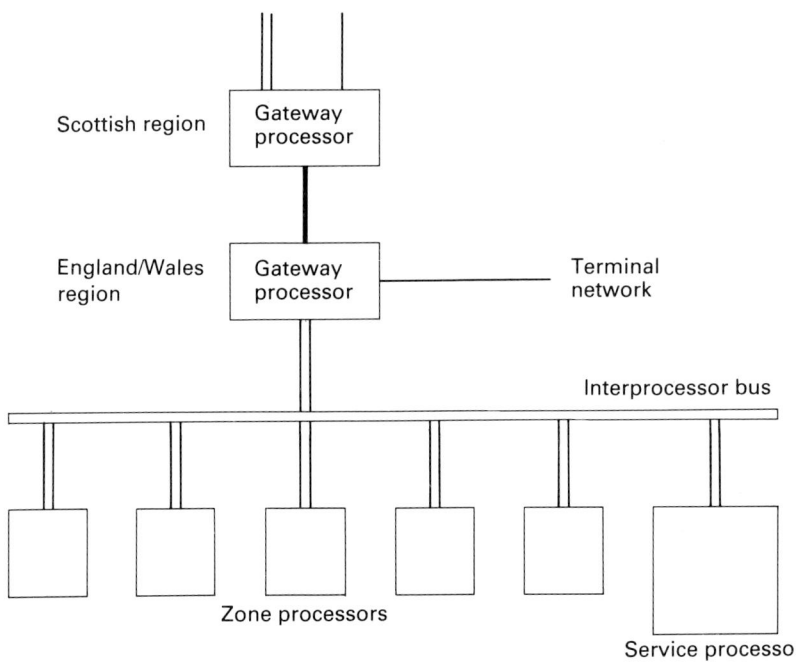

Fig. 7.5 Functional partitioning using gateway processors.

concept to allow for the use of intelligent terminals which package up queries from shops/offices into concise forms for processing at the regional centre.

Our first application partitioning might be considered to be a **vertical** partitioning into partially independent applications. The gateway approach was an example of a partially **horizontal** partitioning where the separate stages of processing through an application were identified. This could be carried further as shown in Fig. 7.6. A combination of these partitioning techniques is likely to be necessary for any realistic application.

There are still a number of alternatives which could be considered in design of a distributed processing system. We have already mentioned the possibility of processing units being installed in the sub-region offices or at individual shops. If we adopt the horizontal partitioning approach then we could, say, place the message handlers in each shop whilst retaining the main processing at the regional centres. The advantage of this approach is that, hopefully, the volume of data transmitted between shops and centre would be reduced; the message handlers would strip out any redundancy.

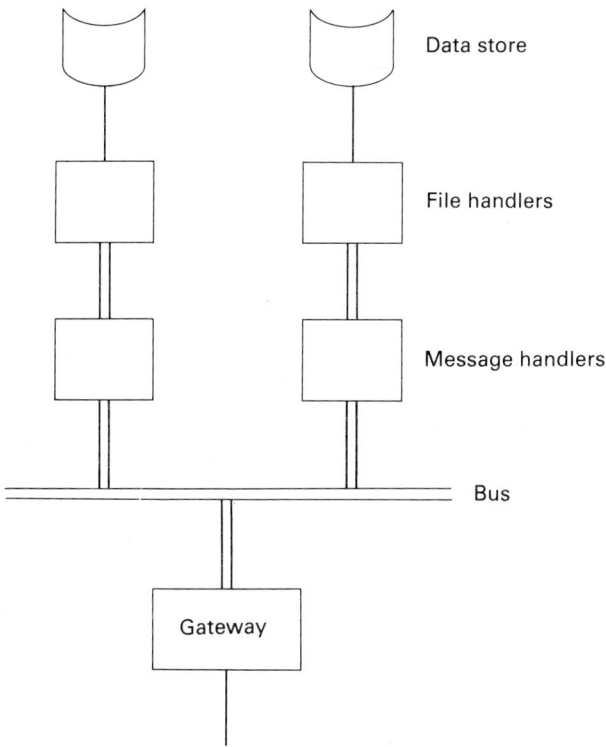

Fig. 7.6 Horizontal partitioning within zone systems.

Disk storage could be shared between sub-region processors. Here we have a trade-off to consider between cost per byte (larger disks being cheaper in this respect) against increased effect of failure and the possibilities of contention.

Another alternative which could be used to reduce the possible effects of failure would be to have duplicate databases at each shop/office. The price we have to pay for this is replication of updating mechanisms and the possibility of information at one site being out of date. The gain is increased reliability in the sense that we are no longer relying on a communication system and a number of processors for response at an individual site. Another modification which might have been adopted to increase reliability is the replication of certain key processors (see Fig. 7.7).

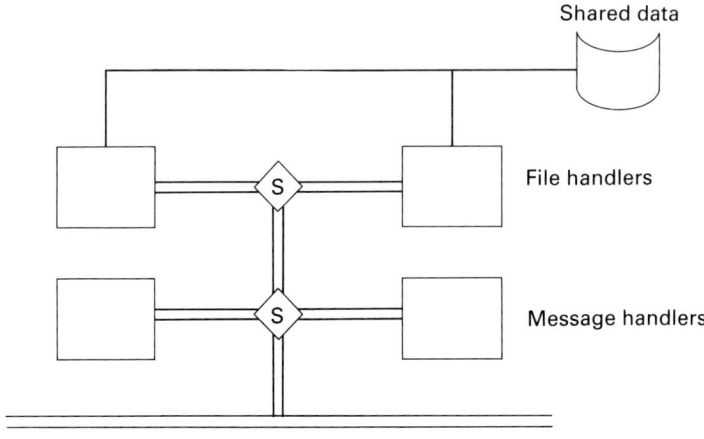

Fig. 7.7 Replication of horizontal partitions for reliability.

Another possible variation is shown in Fig. 7.8. This system has a number of advantages
(1) Replication is across systems not within a system; this has all the advantages of separate power supplies, etc.
(2) Any remote site can get to either system (assuming that this is physically possible — which depends on the geography of the system).
(3) Data replication and synchronization are inherent.
(4) The 'gateway' can contain application logic which makes it more of a front-end processor rather than just a network controller.

To conclude this discussion let us consider a totally different approach. So far we have assumed that we required a system which had to provide a uniform service at each site. Now suppose that our company had one or two large customers. It might be more appropriate to set up a system which could provide these customers with specialized services. Each branch of the company would be controlled by individual managers who might organize the operation in different ways to reflect local needs.

The solution is to define a central **Management Information System** and to give local managers the option of using various systems which all interface with this central facility (see, for example Fig. 7.9).

Designing a Distributed Processing System

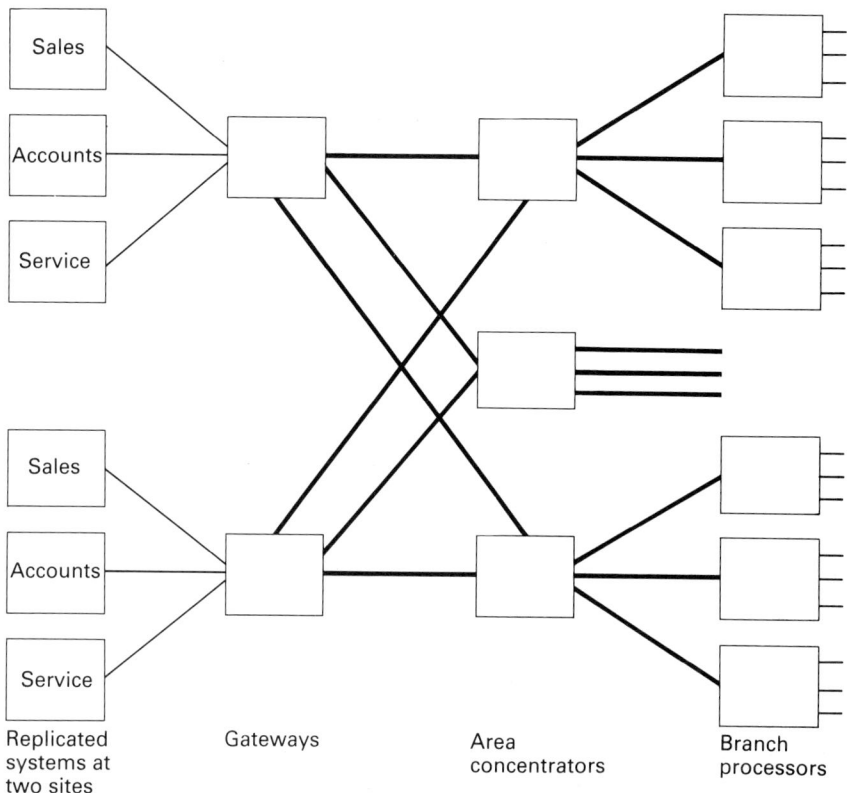

Fig. 7.8 An alternative partitioning involving replication for reliability.

Summary

In this chapter we have illustrated briefly, by means of a simple example, some of the factors which need to be considered in the design of a distributed computing system. We have not attempted to give any hard and fast rules for how to make decisions on what sort of design to use.

Further reading

Further examples of distributed computing systems are discussed by Lorin (1980) and by Weitzmann (1980). Weitzmann's examples contain more implementation details.

88   *Chapter 7*

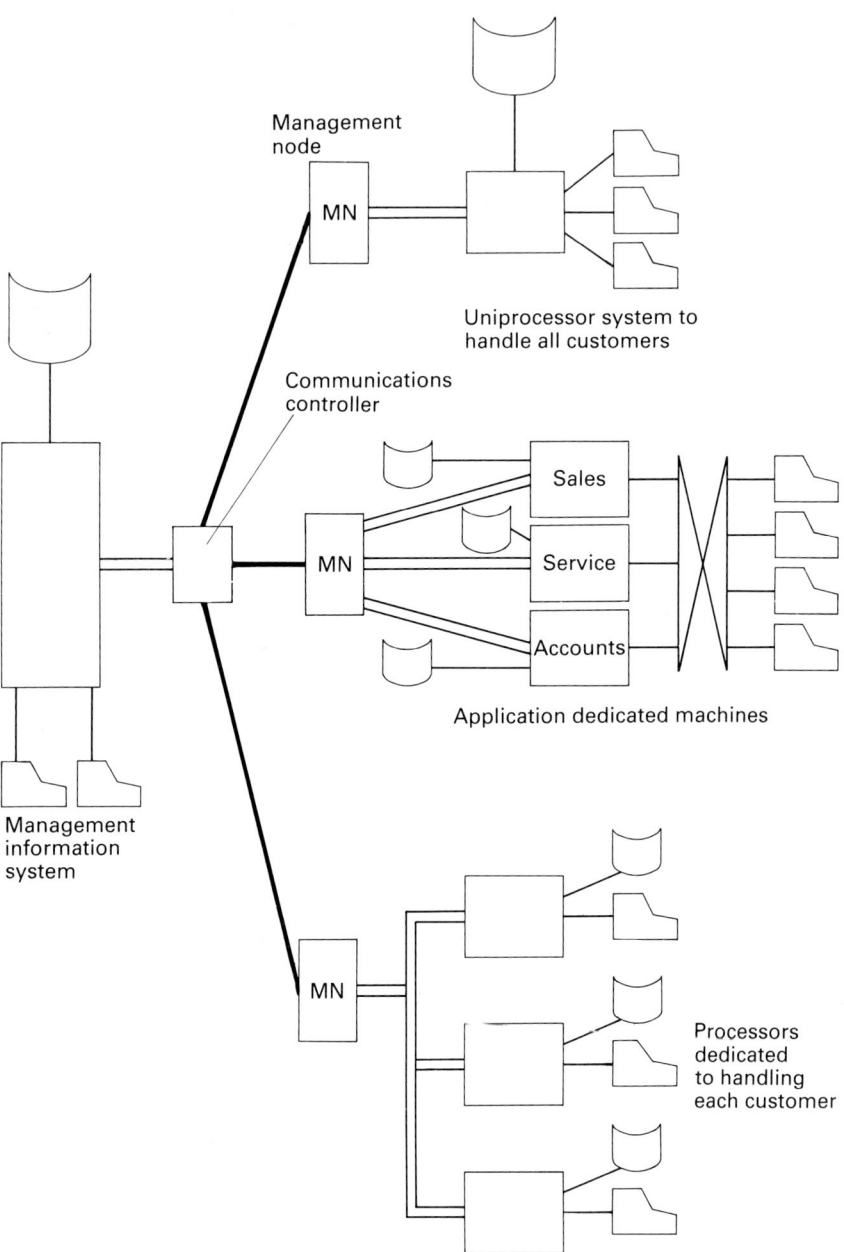

Fig. 7.9 Heterogenous system with local managers having different system structures.

Part 3

Programming for Distributed and Parallel Processing

Apart from noting the facts that a parallel processing system normally implies some distribution of processing, and a distributed processing system normally includes some potential for parallel processing, we have so far discussed parallel and distributed processing systems separately. We have concentrated on the physical characteristics of the two types of system and on how they may logically be regarded as whole systems, rather than as collections of independent processors. In this section the aim is to consider how distributed and parallel processing systems can be programmed.

If we assume that we have a parallel processor of some form then clearly we wish to take advantage of this and exploit all the parallelism which exists in our programs. There are three basic approaches which can be taken and we will examine them all in the next few chapters. If we are considering a distributed processing system then there are two ways in which the way we write programs can be affected.

Firstly, processors may co-operate on the execution of a task. This is the same problem which we are attacking in developing programs for parallel machines except that the level at which parallel processing occurs is going to be much higher in a distributed system.

The second problem comes in to play when we consider the interaction of processes (on logical and/or physical processors) which share some common resource (e.g. parallel updating of a database). This is in fact the same problem which occurs in any multiprocessing system and although, in subsequent chapters, we will mention some of the ways in which this problem can be tackled, the reader is referred to modern operating systems design texts for more detailed discussion.

The first and perhaps most obvious approach to developing parallel programs, and the subject of the next chapter, is to take programs written in an existing language and analyse them to discover how much parallelism they contain and how to exploit it.

The second possibility is to either extend existing languages or define new notations to include specific constructs to express the parallelism and deal with the potential access conflicts (in other words make the programmer do the analysis).

The final option is to define a language which does not include specific parallel constructs, but rather omits the implicit sequencing constructs of existing notations. Thus the analysis is still the province of the compiler/implementation, but the task is made easier. In fact it can be argued that the programmer's task is also made easier, but more of that later.

Chapter 8

Compiling Programs for Parallel Execution

In this chapter we will discuss how programs written in an existing language might be analysed to discover how much parallelism they contain. It is to be hoped that eventually this analysis might be done automatically. For the rest of this chapter we are going to assume that programs are written in some conventional language such as Fortran or Pascal. Even if we eventually consider one of the other approaches to exploiting parallelism in programs more appropriate, this task of analysing traditional programs is worthwhile because of the massive number of existing programs which have been written.

Let us assume that we have a reasonably efficient program. That is, some sensible algorithm has been adopted. We are not in the business of developing new algorithms for parallelism — at least not in this chapter. There are two factors which influence the type of parallel processing which can be done.

The first factor is the type of machine on which we are going to be doing the processing. Some machines are more suited to exploiting one type of parallelism than others. For example, an array processor would clearly be able to speed up the processing of array operations fairly simply, but other forms of parallelism are more difficult to exploit.

The second factor to consider is the basic data structures in the program. The three types of data structure we can consider are

(1) Scalar data — simple numeric constants, etc. These are clearly the easiest to handle in many ways.
(2) Vector data — arrays and strings, etc. which have a regular indexing method. This is the second easiest class to consider.
(3) Other data — complex data structures using pointers, etc. which involve non-regular indexing methods. This class contains all the other data structures you can think of. Eventually we may be able to find sub-classes of this type of data structure which can be handled neatly with various parallel processing techniques, but at the moment very little can be done.

Let us remind ourselves of the various types of computer architecture which have been designed to perform parallel processing. We will be concerned primarily with two characteristics — whether we have just one or multiple processors available and whether each processor operates upon single scalar items of data or upon arrays of data values. The three main classifications we will refer to were introduced in Chapter 4. They are: SEA — single execution array; MEA — multiple execution array; and MES — multiple execution scalar. The fourth category (SES — single execution scalar) does not concern us here as this is the traditional sequential machine.

Loop-free program segments

The simplest form of program to consider is one which does not contain any loops. The two basic forms of statement are the assignment and the conditional.

Let us consider first the assignment. There is a potential for parallelism in evaluating a number of assignments in parallel. We will discuss this possibility later in this chapter when we discuss data dependencies. Let us for the moment concentrate on a single assignment statement. The potential for parallelism lies in the evaluation of the expression on the right hand side. Take as an example a simple expression such as

a+b+c+d+e+f .

When parsed using conventional techniques this would produce a parse tree such as the one in Fig. 8.1a. Evaluation would appear to need $O(n)$ steps. An alternative tree to represent the same expression could be drawn as shown in Fig. 8.1b. Assuming that we have sufficient processing power to perform the additions in parallel this tree would take $O(n)$ steps to

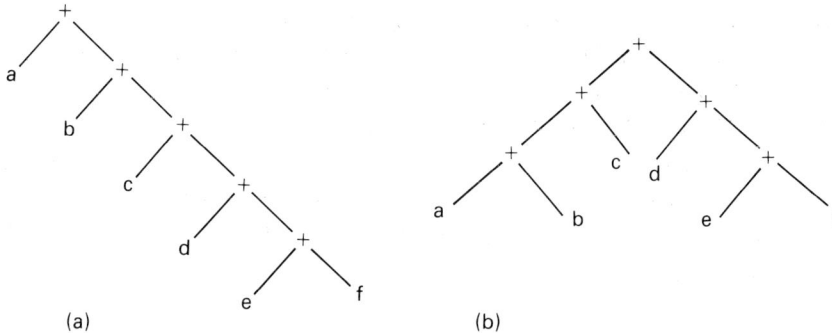

Fig. 8.1 Evaluating a simple expression. (a) Conventional parse requiring $O(n)$ steps; (b) Alternative parse requiring $O(\log n)$ steps.

evaluate. This principle of tree-height reduction is fairly simple to use and can give a reasonable increase in speed for expressions involving scalar data. If the data structures involved are more complex, similar principles can be applied provided that, within the expression, only scalar items of data are used.

The other simple form of statement is the conditional statement. The potential for parallelism here comes from the possibility of evaluating all possible conditions in parallel. For example the statement

```
if <expression 1>
then <statement block 1>
else if <expression 2>
    then <statement block 2>
    else if <expression 3>
        then <statement block 3>
        else <statement block 4>
        fi
    fi
fi
```

involves evaluating three condition expressions. Potentially, these can be done in parallel, thus reducing execution time. Problems can occur if some of the tests in subsequent conditions cause errors if earlier conditions hold. In the following example, the third condition would cause a run-time error if either of the first two conditions hold

```
if i < 1
then writeln('index value too small')
else if i > n
    then writeln('index value too large')
    else if a[i] < 0
        then writeln('selected value is negative')
        else writeln('selected value is positive')
        fi
    fi
fi .
```

It is possible to trap such potential problems, but it does indicate how existing languages are completely indoctrinated by the concept of sequence.

Loops

Virtually all programs contain some form of looping or repetitive computation. Clearly we will be able to achieve great speed gains if we can manage to execute each iteration of a loop in parallel. We will now consider the cases where this might be possible. First of all though, we need to classify the different types of loop which can occur. We will distinguish between loops as represented by some form of loop construct in a program (for while repeat, etc.) and **cycles**.

A loop is said to have a **cycle** if data generated by the body of the loop on one execution of the loop is passed back to the body of the loop on some later execution. Other loops are said to be **acyclic**.

Acyclic loops

A simple example of an acyclic loop is given below

```
for i:=1 to 10
do a[i] := 0
od .
```

Clearly, such loops can be regarded as merely shorthand ways of expressing a number of independent statements which can be evaluated in parallel (using three-height reduction on the expressions as necessary).

If the statement(s) in the body of the loop involve conditions we can associate a bit vector with each assignment to indicate which elements of the vector are to be computed. Consider the following program fragment

```
for i:=1 to 10
do if (i mod 2) = 0 {ie i is even}
    then a[i] := a[i]*2
    else a[i] := 0
    fi
od .
```

Here, a bit vector (F,T,F,T,F,T,F,T,F,T) could be associated with the assignment

a[i] := a[i] * 2

and the complement (T,F,T,F,T,F,T,F,T,F) with the assignment

a[i] := 0.

Both assignments could be executed in parallel over the whole array using the bit vectors to control the execution.

Cyclic loops

Loops with cycles may be split into two categories. Firstly **linear cyclic** loops such as

    for i:= 1 to n
    do x[i]:= a[i]*x[i−1] + b[i]*x[i−2] + c[i]
    od

where the right hand side of the statement is a linear combination of the left hand side variable. The other category of loops is (fairly obviously) **non-linear cycles.**

Linear cyclic loops

Linear cycles are much easier to deal with and we will consider them first. Consider the example we have just given. It may be rewritten in the form

$$x := L x + c$$

where x and c are column vectors and L is an n by n lower triangular matrix containing two sub-diagonals representing the values of the arrays a and b. A typical form of L and c is shown in Fig. 8.2. The **order** m of such a linear system or linear recurrence can be defined as the distance of the farthest non-zero diagonal from the main diagonal (two in this case). This is written as $R<n,m>$. The solution of the recurrence (x) can be expressed as the product of n matrices (each containing one column of L and c). This standard product-form algorithm can be used to evaluate linear recurrences of lower order in a fast and efficient manner. As the order grows the number of processors required to obtain useful speed-up becomes too large for this approach to be efficient. Nevertheless SEA and MES machines can be used efficiently on lower order problems using this approach.

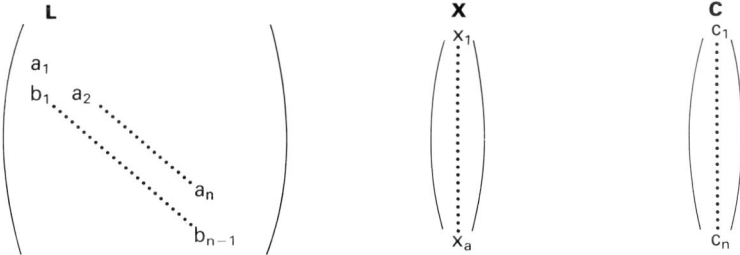

Fig. 8.2 Matrices for performing linear cyclic loops.

Chapter 8

Since this algorithm becomes rather inefficient at higher orders we will consider some alternative approaches for some particular types of linear cyclic loops. Consider the loop below which uses two-dimensional arrays

```
for i:=1 to n
do      for j:=1 to n
        do      x[i,j] := x[i-1,j]+x[i,j-1]+c
        od
od .
```

If this loop is rewritten for a one-dimensional array we end up with a product form algorithm of the order $R<n^2,n>$. An alternative is to use what is known as a wavefront algorithm. This requires re-indexing the array as shown in Fig. 8.3. The loop can then be rewritten

```
for i:=1 to n
do      in parallel with j=1 to i
        do      x[i,j]:=x[x[i-1,j]+x[i-1,j-1]+c
        od
od;
k:=2;
for i:=n+1 to 2*n-1
do      in parallel with j=k to n
        do      k:=k+1;
                x[i,j]:=x[i-j]+x[i-1,j-1]+c
        od
od .
```

This method of using a wavefront algorithm is effective on SEA machines for arrays with two or more dimensions as we are able to compute simultaneously all the elements of lower dimension arrays which appear in the program.

On an MES machine we can use the wavefront approach if a linear recurrence occurs in a loop along with many other statements. Consider the following example which also uses the technique known as **loop distribution**. Suppose we had the loop below

```
for i:=1 to n
do      x[i,1] := x[i-1,1]+ x[i,0] + c;
        x[i,2] := x[i-1,2] + x[i,1] + c;
            ⋮
        x[i,n] := x[i-1,n] + x[i,n-1] + c
od .
```

Compiling Programs for Parallel Execution

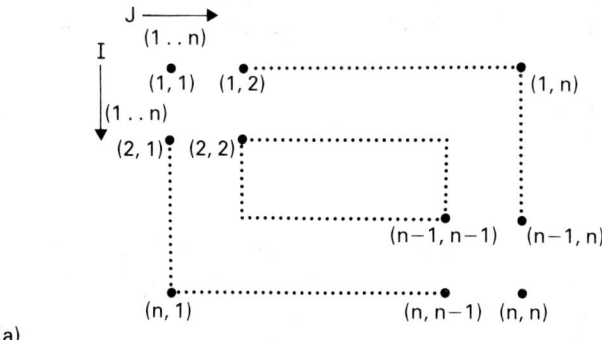

(a)

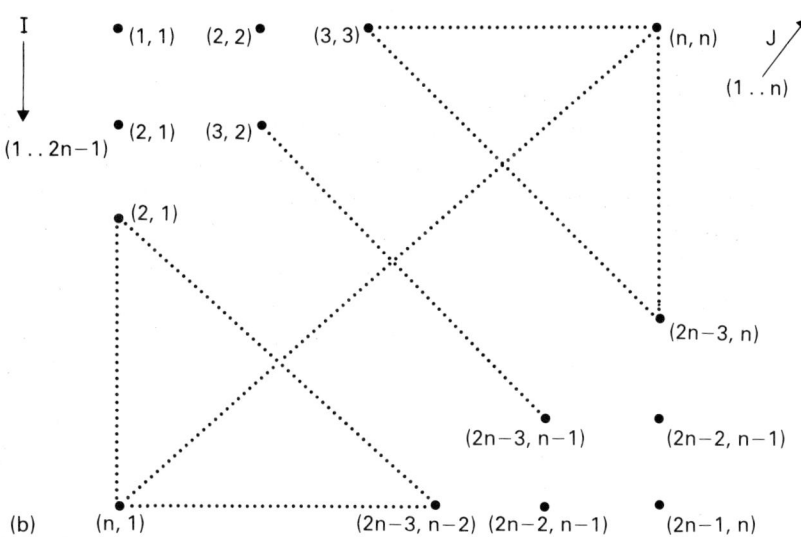

(b)

Fig. 8.3 Re-indexing arrays for use with wavefront algorithm. (a) Original array; (b) Re-indexed array.

We can rewrite this as a number of loops

```
for i:=1 to n
do      x[i,i] := x[i−1,1] + x[i,0] + c
od
```

$$\vdots$$

```
for i:=1 to n
do      x[i,n] := x[i−1,n] + x[i,n−1] + c .
od .
```

Assigning one processor to each loop gives us the execution pattern illustrated in Fig. 8.4. The number of time steps required is $2*n-1$, provided that we have sufficient processors available.

Non-linear cyclic loops

We will now turn to the most difficult form of loop to speed up; those containing non-linear cycles. There is no general solution to loops of this type, so we will restrict ourselves to making a few general comments.

(1) It is possible to rewrite some algorithms which contain non-linear recurrences into ones which contain only linear recurrences. This should be done if possible.
(2) There are some algorithms, such as sorting and merging, which can be tackled by formulating them directly on to parallel hardware. Some examples of this will be seen later.
(3) For SEA machines it is sometimes possible to interchange the order of loop indexing on non-linear recurrences to get the non-linear indexes to the outermost loop(s). The inner loop(s) can then be speeded up using the techniques for linear cycles outlined earlier.
(4) Similar techniques to the loop distribution method just described can be used on MES machines for various non-linear recurrences to achieve a speed-up proportional to the number of cycles occurring in its loop. This approach is essentially a form of pipelining. It should be noted however that the synchronization and data communication problems in adopting this approach may be very complex.

So far we have only considered very small program fragments and have found ways of executing what are essentially single statements in parallel.

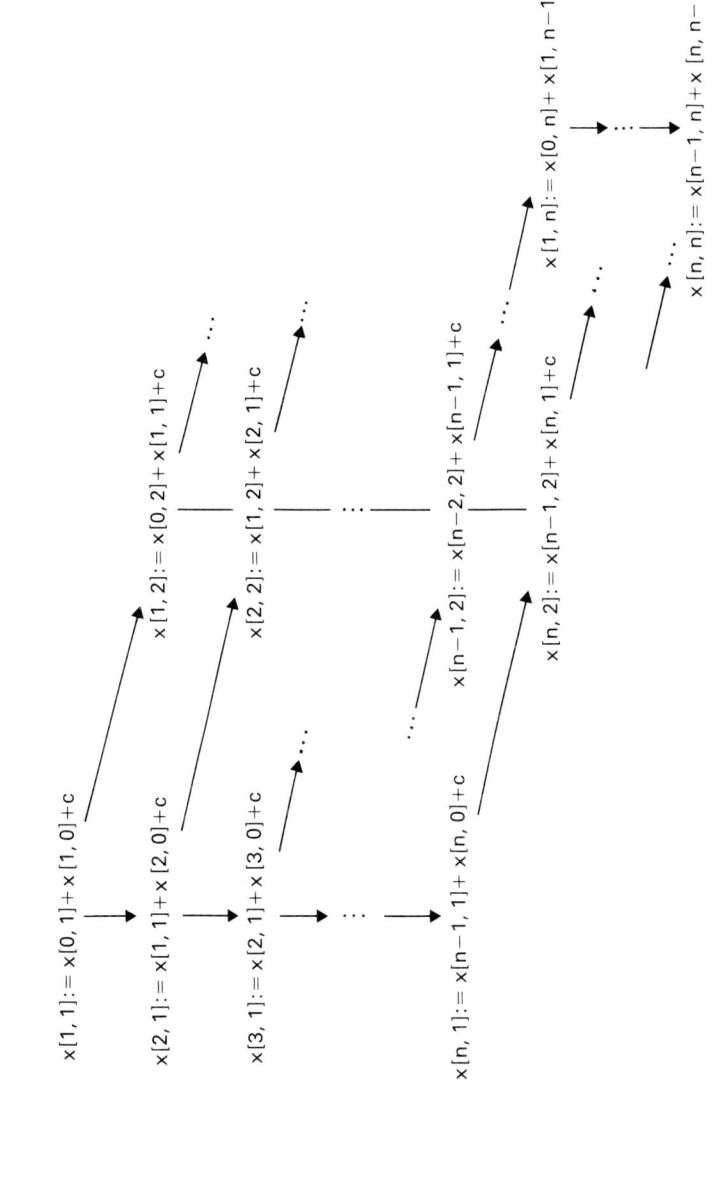

Fig. 8.4 Wavefront algorithm on n processors. (Arrows show flow dependencies).

A more complicated problem is removing cyclic dependencies. Consider the simple program below

```
           for 1:=1 to n
           do      for j:=1 to m
S1                 do      c[i] := x[i] + 1;
S2                         a := c[i] + 1
                   od
           od
```

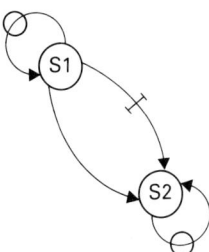

Fig. 8.7 Original dependencies.

which gives rise to the dependencies illustrated in Fig. 8.7. By expanding the one-dimensional vectors a and c into two-dimensional arrays we obtain the following equivalent program fragment

```
           for 1:=1 to n
           do      for j:=1 to m
S1'                do      cl[i,j] := x[i] + 1;
S2'                        al[i,j] := c[i,j] + 1
                   od
           od;
S3'        a := al[n,m];
S4'        c[] := cl[ ,m]
```

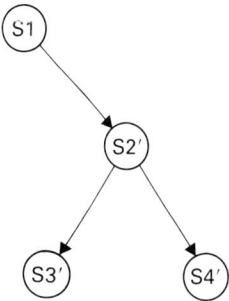

Fig. 8.8 Dependencies after cycle removal.

which gives the dependency relationships shown in Fig. 8.8. Now we have no cyclic dependencies and each iteration of the loop can be executed in parallel.

Next let us consider the problem of cyclic dependencies involving control dependency. As a simple example, consider the program below

```
           for i:=1 to n
S1         do      p[i] := a[i−1] > 0;
                   if p[i]
S2                 then a[i] := c[i]
                   fi
           od
```

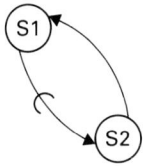

Fig. 8.9 A control dependency cycle.

which gives the dependency graph shown in Fig. 8.9. This loop can be replaced by two loops as below

```
           for i:=1 to n
S1'        do      p[i] := (p[i−1] and (c[i−1] > 0)) or (not p[i−1] and (a[i−1] > 0 ))
           od;
           for i:=1 to n
           do      if p[i]
S2'                then a[i] := c[i]
                   fi
           od .
```

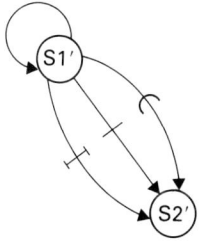

Fig. 8.10 Dependency graph after cycle removal.

The dependency graph then becomes that shown in Fig. 8.10. We still have a cyclic dependency on statement S1, but there is no cyclic dependency on S2. S1 is in fact an example of a form of statement termed a **boolean recurrence** which can often be recognized by a compiler and executed in parallel.

Principles of graph abstraction

So far we have given a few simple examples of graph transformations to allow for an increase in parallel execution. Some machines have special features which can help and we will now mention briefly some of these. First though, let us assume that our compiler has built us a complete dependence graph; that we have transformed it using the general techniques outlined earlier to remove as many arcs as possible and that we have distributed loop control so that loops consist only of simple cycles or single nodes in the graph.

Some cycles such as summing a vector can be replaced by single reduction instructions which exist on some machines (e.g. CRAY-1, CYBER 203/205). Some machines (e.g. Burroughs BSP) have special instructions to solve first order linear recurrences. Well-known linear recurrence algorithms for multiple ALU machines also exist.

Therefore, if we replace flow dependency cycles by recurrence nodes then in many cases we have solved our problem. Similar techniques can be applied to other forms of dependency (e.g. output and anti-) if we treat them as flow dependencies.

Another useful technique is that of **node fusion.** Suppose we have two nodes with identical index sets. Depending upon certain dependency conditions it is possible to fuse these nodes to give a common loop control node. This removes various forms of input dependencies and is effective in restricting the use of critical resources at run-time. For example, in a virtual memory system this approach allows the multiple use of a page which has been fetched from secondary memory.

If we adopt all the above techniques then we end up with a directed acyclic graph (dag). Nodes in each anti-chain of a dag can be executed simultaneously. Recurrence algorithms can be selected in accordance with the type of architecture being used, the resources available and the scheduling algorithm for tasks being adopted. In some cases tree-height reduction can be applied to expressions to improve the performance.

Summary and further reading

We have examined a number of techniques for speeding up the processing of programs written in a conventional sequential language by finding steps which can be potentially executed in parallel. This can be done within an expression by techniques such as tree-height reduction; within loop statements by techniques such as loop unrolling or vectorization; and between statements by analysing the data dependencies. We have also noted briefly some special techniques which can be applied depending upon the architecture of particular machines. Many of these techniques are discussed in more detail by Kuck in Evans (1982).

We have not discussed the ways in which algorithms can be developed to make use of parallel architectures. To do this effectively we need a good appreciation of the particular application area. Most of the work which has been done in this field has related to large scale numerical applications. The interested reader is recommended to refer either to the chapters in Evans (1982) written by Professor Evans himself or to one of the following collections of articles: Feilmeier (1977), Rodriguez (1982), Feilmeier *et al.* (1984) and Paddon (1984).

Chapter 9

Programming for Array Processors

In the last chapter we looked at the various ways in which a sequential program could be speeded up by finding all the potential for parallel processing. In doing the analysis we assumed that we had a sensible sequential algorithm to start with. In many cases we actually need to redesign the algorithm in order to make use of the potential parallel processing capability of the hardware. This is particularly true of the array processor where problems have to be recast in terms of operations on whole arrays. In the case of the ICL DAP there is also the problem of working with 1-bit processors. Most users will not actually have to worry about this aspect as a high-level language is used which hides such features. Nevertheless, it is useful to have an appreciation of the implications which such features have on the performance of programs.

The subject of this chapter is therefore an introduction to the design and implementation of algorithms for an array processor. We will restrict ourselves to considering the ICL DAP as an example. We will also restrict ourselves to a few simple example algorithms which nevertheless serve to illustrate how conventional ideas of efficiency cannot be carried over to array processors in a straightforward way. Initially, we will present our algorithms using the assembly level programming language of the DAP. Later, we will see how a high-level language can be used. Since this is not intended to be an introduction to actually programming the DAP, but rather a discussion of the principles involved, we may occasionally use rather imprecise syntax.

We start our discussion by looking at a routine to add two 16-bit integers. Since the processing units in the DAP are 1-bit processors this is not as trivial an example as it might first appear. Note how the following assembly language level program requires a loop in order to perform even this simple operation

Programming for Array Processors

```
               !There are 3 registers M1 M2 M3
               !M1 and M2 point to most significant bits
               !of fields to be added.
               !M3 to point to most significant bit of answer.

               CF                        !initialize carry to false in all PEs
               DO        16 TIMES
               QS        0.15(M1-)       !load least significant bit of field M1
                                         !into Q and decrement register (-)
               CQPCQS    0.15(M2-)       !add contents of C Q and bit 15 of M2
                                         !together and leave result in C and Q
                                         !decrement register
    LOOP:      SQ        0.15(M3-)       !store least significant bit
                                         !decrement register.
```

As we mentioned in Chapter 4 this leads to some rather interesting relative timings for operations. In particular the level of precision required affects the timings (the number of iterations of the loop is proportional to the precision) and arithmetic is relatively slow compared to data movement.

Bearing these points in mind we will now turn to a more interesting example. Here we are interested in finding which processor's memory contains the largest of a set of values. Traditionally this problem would require a number of comparisons between integer values. Comparisons are often thought of as subtractions followed by a sign test. If a $>$ b then (a–b) is positive, a $<$ b implies (a–b) is negative and a= b implies (a–b) is zero. In the DAP we adopt a rather different approach. The principle is that we assume initially that all processing elements (PEs) are candidates for having the largest value. At each stage of the process we eliminate those PEs which can no longer possibly contain the largest value. This is done by setting the activity register to indicate if a PE is a candidate for containing the largest value. At each stage we eliminate all those PEs whose value does not have a 1 in the most significant place (currently being considered). We then pass along the values looking at each bit in order of significance. The only catch is that we have to check that at no stage do we eliminate all possible PEs. This can occur if all contenders at any stage have a zero bit. If this does occur we just reset the pattern of activity bits (contenders) to the previous pattern and carry on. At the end, all those PEs whose A-registers are set to one contain a copy of the largest value. An assembly language program to do this is given below

```
          !M1 points to most significant bit of value in each PE
       AT                  !set all activity bits to true
                           !(all PEs are candidates for containing
                           ! maximum value)
       QA                  !note contents of A in register Q
       DO      32 TIMES    !repeat for all bits in data
       AMS     0.0(M1+ )   !logical and of A register and bit pointed
                           !at by M1. Increment M1
       RANO    M4          !and all columns of inverse A registers
                           !and place result in M4
       SKIP    ALL M4 0    !test if all bits of M4 are zero
       AQ                  !reset A to previous pattern (stored in Q)
LOOP:  QA                  !store current contents of A in Q .
```

Let us now try to analyse the performance of the DAP in comparison with traditional processors, taking this searching program as an example. Two terms which are often defined are **speed-up** and **efficiency.** If we write the time taken for P processors to execute a task as Tp, then we can define **speed-up** to be Sp = T1/Tp . **Efficiency** can be defined as Ep = Sp/p . This value is always less than one, but we hope to get as close to one as possible.

In trying to use these measures on the DAP we have to try and say how long it would take to perform a task on one processor. This is meaningless for the searching problem as the algorithm depends upon there being more than one processor. Let us have a look at efficiency in other terms then. It could be defined as the proportion of the processing power which is being used in any task. Our searching example takes a maximum of 16 iterations for 16-bit data (assuming that if at an earlier stage we reduce the number of candidates to one we stop — this code is not included in the assembly language version). Therefore we have a potential of 16 × 64 × 64 processing cycles available. On the first iteration we therefore use 64 × 64 processing cycles. At each iteration it is probably reasonable to assume that we eliminate about half of the possible values. Subsequent iterations therefore use 32 × 64, 16 × 64, 8 × 64, 4 × 64, 2 × 64, 64, 32, 16, 8, 4, 2 and 1 processing cycle. This gives us a utilization measure of 4096 + 2048 + 1024 + 512 + 256 + 128 + 64 + 32 + 16 + 8 + 4 + 2 + 1 cycles used out of a possible 13 × 4096 (= 53 248). We therefore utilize 8191/53 248 = 15% of the potential processor capacity. This does not appear to be very efficient, but our searching algorithm takes less time than a simple addition or multiplication! This would seem to suggest that it ought to be a very good algorithm. Clearly the traditional measures of speed-up and efficiency which may be applicable to multiprocessor systems are totally inapplicable to the DAP.

One lesson to be learned from this example is that programming a DAP requires the user to look at problems in a new way. The comparative performance figures also suggest that we ought to re-examine our basic assumptions about what is 'efficient'. The fact that certain things take a long time (floating point multiplications, searches, etc.) is hardware dependent and not a fixed rule of arithmetic.

So far we have seen how an array processor can be programmed at a low level. Now we will examine briefly some of the extensions to high-level languages which are required in order to program array processors. We will take as our example the version of FORTRAN used to program the ICL DAP (known, fairly obviously, as DAP-FORTRAN). It is common for FORTRAN to be the basis for extending languages for array processors as it is still the most widely used language in scientific and numerical applications. It would be equally possible to provide extensions for languages such as Pascal, C, Algol 68, etc., but none of these languages has been widely accepted by the numerical computation community who are the main users of array processors.

The first obvious extension is to extend the set of possible data types to include array and vector types suitable for use on the array processor. The sizes of these types are dependent upon the size of a particular array processor. For the ICL DAP at Queen Mary College the two new types are vectors (of 64 elements) and matrices (of 4096 elements = 64 × 64). Having defined these types the standard arithmetic operations are defined to work on such types. Thus it is perfectly possible to write X = Y + Z, where X, Y and Z are all vectors or matrices and X is the element by element sum of Y and Z,. The expression Y*Z would mean the element by element multiplication of Y and Z, not the matrix multiplication of Y and Z. As well as arithmetic operations, comparison operations can be extended to apply to matrices and vectors. For example the expression (Y.GE.0) where Y is a matrix, produces a 64 × 64 bit map of true values where $Y(i,i)$ is greater than zero and false values elsewhere. This sort of logical masking is a powerful tool which can be used cheaply as it can make use of the activity register of the DAP. The mask is simply used to set the values of the A registers. This is one advantage of a 1-bit architecture.

Earlier we saw how a routine to find all the maximum values in an array of values could be found, written in a low-level language. In a high-level language it would be written as

```
        LOGICAL MATRIX FUNCTION MAXP(INP_DATA)
        INTEGER INP_DATA( ,)
        LOGICAL BITS_OF_INP( ,,32)
        EQUIVALENCE (INP_DATA, BITS OF_INP( ,,1))
        MAXP = .NOT. BITS_OF_INP( ,,1)
        DO 1 I = 2, 32
                IF (ANY(MAXP .AND. BITS_OF_INP( ,,I))
     *                  MAXP .AND. BITS_OF_INP( ,,I)
    1   CONTINUE
        RETURN
        END .
```

A number of points about this code are worth commenting upon
(1) Function definitions have been extended to include the matrix and vector types. That is, functions can return values of these types.
(2) The sizes of arrays and matrices are machine specified so they can be defined by omission (see lines 2 and 3).
(3) The equivalence statement of FORTRAN is used to select those bits we are interested in.
(4) We have a function ANY which is a logical OR of all the bits in a matrix.

Of course such a simple routine is supplied as a library function (written in machine code). The function returning the positions of maximum values is called MAXP and takes about 32μs. The version which returns the value is called MAXV and takes about 50μs to execute.

Another useful operation is illustrated by the mesh function

$$Q(i,j) = (P(i,j+1) + P(i-1,j) + P(i+1,j) + P(i,j-1))/4$$

for all i,j. This would normally be implemented by using two nested loops iterating through the values of i and j. In DAP-FORTRAN we hve a concept of shift indexing

$$Q = 0.25*(P(,+) + P(-,) + P(+,) + P(,-)) .$$

The only problem remaining is what to do at the edges. Two options are available: **cyclic connectivity** where each row and column is considered to wrap around to the edge value at the opposite end and **plane connectivity** where all values outside the matrix are assumed to have a zero value.

A common application of array processors is matrix manipulation which involves matrix multiplication. Figure 9.1 illustrates three versions of a matrix multiplication program. Version (a) is the conventional sequential program. Version (b) illustrates how some parallelism can be

```
DO  1   I=1, N
DO  1   J=1, N
    C(I, J)=0.0
    DO  1   K=1, N
    C(I, J)=C(I, J)+A(I, K)*B(K, J)
1. CONTINUE
(a)

DO  2   I=1, N
DO  2   J=1, N
C(I, J)=0.0
2. CONTINUE
DO  1   K=1, N
DO  1   I=1, N
DO  1   J=1, N
C(I, J)=C(I, J)+A(I, K)*B(K, J)
1. CONTINUE
(b)

C=0.0
DO  1   K=1, N
C=C+MATC(A(, K))* MATR(B(K, ))
1  CONTINUE
(c)
```

Fig. 9.1 Matrix multiplication. (a) Sequential matrix multiplication; (b) Introducing parallelism by separating out loops; (c) A DAP-FORTRAN version using expansion operators.

introduced by separating the loops out and version (c) is the DAP-FORTRAN version using the functions MATC and MATR which take array vectors and create matrices whose columns or rows respectively are all copies of that vector. These functions are termed expansion operators.

Let us consider some timings for the above algorithms. For the serial FORTRAN version we have three nested loops each done N times so our time is proportional to N^3. The parallel version requires only one loop provided that we have at least N^2 processors. This gives a time proportional to N. The ratio of the speed of the parallel solution compared to the speed of the serial solution is a function of the size of the problem.

If we have a 64 × 64 matrix, life is easy and we have maximum speed-up. If we have a 128 × 128 matrix this is all right as we merely split the matrix into four sections. The speed-up is not as great but we still have a significant increase in speed. If, on the other hand, our matrix is say only 3 × 3 or 66 × 66, then we have problems. Unfortunately with an array processor the only solution is to attempt to recast the problem in terms of the right size of arrays (i.e. 64 × 64).

Summary

We have attempted to illustrate some of the ways in which languages can be adapted to enable programs to be written for array processors. We have concentrated on the ICL DAP as an extreme example of an array processor. If each PE in the array is more powerful and/or operates on a larger word size, then some of our arguments become less valid. One question to be asked is: can potential gain in speed of simple arithmetic operations (which is what more powerful PEs implies) be utilized usefully? We have already seen that processor utilization figures do not seem particularly applicable to array processors. If each element is only a very cheap simple processor, low utilization is nothing to worry about. If each processor is larger and is closer to what might be used in a true multiprocessor, then perhaps we have to question the whole array processor approach.

This chapter has, hopefully, indicated that some problems which initially do not appear suited to array processing may indeed be amenable to such methods. Any APL programmer will need little convincing of that for many APL one-liners rely on manipulating vectors and matrices as whole objects. It might be argued that rather than adapting strictly sequential languages such as FORTRAN we ought to have looked at compiling APL for array processors. This is unfortunately outside the scope of the current text.

The extensions to FORTRAN we have discussed in this chapter are examples of ways in which conventional languages can be extended to cater for parallel processing in a rather restricted form. In the next chapter we will look at some further extensions which allow for more general parallel processing such as can be performed on multiprocessors.

Further reading

Much of the material included in this chapter is based on Parkinson's excellent introduction to the practical ways in which array processors can be used which can be found in Evans (1982).

Chapter 10

Programming with Shared Memory

In this chapter we will introduce some of the extensions which have been suggested to enable programmers to make use of parallel processing facilities when the parallel processors share common memory. The emphasis will therefore be on synchronizing access to this shared memory. Let us begin, though, by simply looking at how we might add the concept of parallel execution to a conventional sequential language.

The most obvious approach is to introduce an alternative to the strict sequence operation (usually represented in most languages by semicolon). Usually blocks bracketed by symbols such as **parbegin** and **parend** or **cobegin** and **coend** are used, e.g.

cobegin
        statement_one;
        statement_two;
          :
        statement_n
coend .

It is perfectly possible, however, to replace the semicolon by a comma in the way that Algol 68 uses collateral clauses

    (statement_one, statement_two, ... , statement_n) .

This restricts our parallelism to the statement level. To introduce parallel blocks of code a notation such as **fork** and **join** is required, e.g.

        :
    fork label;
        :
    process one
        :
    join;
label: statement;
        :
    process two
        :
    quit; .

Often, forking is regarded as producing a second child process which then terminates by executing a quit command. The original process which contained the fork instruction carries on (as the parent process) and waits for termination of the child process by executing a join. A third option is that of communicating sequential processors, which we will deal with in more detail in a later chapter.

The simple **cobegin coend** model allows us to introduce the concept of concurrent processes. Each statement within a block is a separate process. If we allow procedure calls to be included then this is more obvious. If the concurrent processes use no common data they are said to be **disjoint** or **independent**. A simple example of this is the program fragment below

>   **cobegin**
>   >   m1 := max(a, b);
>   >   m2 := max(c, d)
>
>   **coend**;
>   >   m := max(m1, m2) .

This is the easiest form of concurrency to control, but there may be times when life is not so simple. Consider the following two examples. The results of these computations depend upon the relative speed of the processes. The values of j and count will depend on the order in which the two processes access the variables

>   >   j := 10;
>   >   **cobegin**
>   >   >   writeln(j);
>   >
>   >   **coend**

>   observer: while true
>   >   do   observe an event;
>   >   >   count := count = 1
>   >
>   >   od

>   reporter: while true
>   >   do   writeln(count);
>   >   >   count := 0
>   >
>   >   od .

Programming with Shared Memory

These parts of the computation are said to be **time critical**. We refer to the concept of the result depending upon the speeds as a **race condition**. Such problems only occur if we have either true parallel processing (on separate CPUs) or logical concurrency (with a time-sliced CPU). An alternative to the obvious solution of insisting that all concurrent processes are disjoint is to identify the particular parts of the processes which cause the problem. We need to ensure that only one process at a time may access shared data which is updated. Strictly speaking, we only need to ensure sole access for updating. At other times multiple reads are possible without any potential for corrupt results. The parts of the processes which perform the updates are termed **critical sections** and the required access is said to be **mutually exclusive.**

Consider the example below where the critical sections are indicated by the keywords **mutexbegin** and **mutexend**

```
process P1:
    while not finished
    do    use variables local to P1;
          mutexbegin
                  access shared variables
          mutexend;
          use variables local to P1
    od

process P2:
    while not finished
    do    use variables local to P2;
          mutexbegin
                  access shared variables
          mutexend
          use variables local to P2
    od .
```

A simple extension to this concept is to allow the critical section to refer to specific shared variables by putting them as parameters to mutexbegin and mutexend. This is particularly useful if a number of shared variables are accessed in a number of critical sections. We would not want to restrict processing in two critical sections which access different variables.

Let us now consider how we might implement the concept of critical sections. Every time a mutexbegin is encountered the process must determine if there is any other process in a critical section; i.e. has another process passed a mutexbegin, but not the corresponding mutexend? If this is the case then the entering process must wait until no other process is in the critical section. On passing beyond the mutexbegin the process must set an indicator so that other processes reaching a mutexbegin will wait.

On reaching a mutexend the process must allow a waiting process (if any) to enter the critical section. An obvious implementation would be

mutexbegin:
>   while occupied
>   do skip
>   od;
>   occupied := true

mutexend:
>   occupied := false.

Unfortunately these two processes refer to a shared variable 'occupied' which must be accessed by mutually exclusive processes (using mutexbegin and mutexend!). In order to solve this problem, we require a hardware facility known as **memory interlock** which allows multiple processors to access memory in a mutually exclusive fashion. The memory device receives fetch and store commands from numerous processors, but only executes one command at once. Let us consider again our simple example involving the updating and printing of a value j

>   j := 10;
>   **cobegin**
>   writeln(j);
>   j := 1000;
>   **coend** .

Without memory interlock the value of j printed would be a random bit pattern consisting of parts of the bit pattern for 10 and parts of the bit pattern for 1000. With memory interlock we would get either the value 10 or the value 1000. This is clearly what we need to implement our mutexbegin. However, it is not sufficient to replace mutexbegin as more than one operation often needs to be carried out in a critical section.

Our simple algorithms are still not quite adequate. The implementation of mutexbegin makes a test of the flag occupied and if it is false then sets it to true. Unfortunately there is nothing to stop another process accessing the flag occupied in between these two steps and also entering the critical section. An alternative is the implementation below

Programming with Shared Memory

mutexbegin:
    while turn <> my_turn
    do skip
    od

mutexend:
    turn := his_turn .

This has the unfortunate property of enforcing alternation between the two processes. If this is not required then we need to adopt something like Dekker's algorithm

mutexbegin:
    need[me] := true;
    while need[other]
    do   if turn <> me
        then need[me] := false;
                while turn <> me
                do skip
                od;
                need[me] := true
        fi
    od

mutexend:
    need[me] := false;
    turn := other .

In order to convince yourself that this works it is suggested that you work through a few examples. This algorithm has the following properties
(1) Only one process at a time in the critical section.
(2) A process is allowed to enter the critical section only if no other process is already in it.
(3) No processor is kept waiting indefinitely to enter a critical section. (There is in fact a theoretical set of timings which violate this, but for all practical purposes this property holds.)

If we are fortunate in our choice of hardware all the above contortions may prove unnecessary. If the instruction set contains a single instruction of the form testandset, which tests the value of an operand and sets a value to it in one operation, then we can implement the simple algorithms for mutexbegin and mutexend we had earlier

testandset(operand) performs in one operation:
    return value of (code = operand)
    operand := true

mutexbegin:
    testandset(occupied);
    while code
    do testandset(occupied)
    od

mutexend:
    occupied := false .

An example of such an instruction is a decrement instruction which sets a condition flag if the answer is negative.

It is worth pointing out that all the above methods of implementing critical sections use a technique known as **busy waiting.** That is, the processor which is waiting to enter the critical section is continuously testing a flag to see if it is permitted to enter. This is acceptable only if processor time is cheap or if critical sections are executed for comparatively small amounts of time. If this is not the case then we would need to investigate the possibilities of processors becoming idle when waiting to enter a critical section and being reawoken only when another process exits from a critical section. This is particularly important if we are implementing our concurrent processes using a time-sliced CPU. One possible approach which uses this concept is the use of **semaphores.** The basic form of semaphore, S, is a two-valued variable shared by all the processes which wish to access a critical region. Only two operations are allowed on the semaphore. These operations must be carried out as indivisible operations. They are

(1) The **wait** operation — P(s).

Wait until s is greater than 0; then subtract 1 from s.

(2) The **signal** operation — v(s).

Add 1 to S.

The semaphore is initialized to 1 and a process executes a P operation before entering a critical region, and a v operation on leaving it.

Having defined what a simple semaphore is, we turn to the question of how to implement it. A semaphore is in fact simply the occupied variable which we used to implement mutexbegin and mutexend if we had a single test and set operation. In fact, if we declare a semaphore mutex then P(mutex) implements mutexbegin and v(mutex) implements mutexend.

If the processes share CPU time by time-slicing then semaphores are implemented by using a software-kernel (a shared sub-routine which accesses the semaphores). When a process is blocked by a P operation, rather than implement a busy waiting strategy it can allocate the CPU to a ready process.

We have seen that mutexbegin and mutexend can be implemented using semaphores. The reverse is true, we can implement semaphores using mutexbegin and mutexend

v(s):
>> **mutexbegin**
>> >> s := s + 1
>> **mutexend**

P(s):
>> blocked := true;
>> while blocked
>> do   **mutexbegin**
>> >> if s > 0
>> >> then   s := s − 1;
>> >> >> blocked := false
>> >> fi
>> >> **mutexend**
>> od .

Another common synchronization primitive which has been proposed is the use of **block/wake-up** facilities. Here processes are considered to wait (block) until activated by another process (wake-up), as illustrated below for two processes Q and R

Q   compute:
>> **wake-up** R;
>> compute:
>> >> :
>> >> :

R: compute;
>> **block** until awakened by Q;
>> compute;
>> >> :
>> >> :

These facilities can be implemented using semaphores. Each process involved is associated with one semaphore from a vector of semaphores (say privsems) and each process knows the address of its own entry (say me). All the semaphores are initialized to zero to indicate that they are awaiting a wake-up command. A call to wake-up (process-id) could then be implemented by the command v(privsems[process-id]). The command p(privsem[me]) would execute a block command.

Let us now consider an example and see how it might be implemented using semaphores. We have a number of processes which share a number of identical resources (e.g. tape-drives). We assume that there are insufficient resources to assign one to each process. When a process requires access to a resource it executes a request command and when it has finished with a resource it executes a release command. In order to implement this using a binary semaphore system, we define a single semaphore (access), a variable (avail) to contain a count of available resources and a queue of process-ids to contain process-ids of processes waiting to gain access to a resource. We also need a vector of semaphores (one for each process) (proclist) in order to determine which waiting process is allocated a resource next.

The request routine also requires a local boolean variable blocked. The code for a request is

```
p(access);
blocked := avail = 0;
if      blocked
then    put this process's process-id into waiting queue
else    avail := avail −1;
        allocate resource
fi;
v(access);
if      blocked
then    p(proclist[this process-id])
fi .
```

The release routine is

```
P(access);
release resource;
avail := avail + 1;
find U the process-id of the head of the waiting queue;
if     U exists
then   remove U from queue;
       allocate resource to U;
       avail := avail - 1;
       v(proclist[U])
fi;
v(access) .
```

It should be noted that mutexbegin and mutexend could be used instead of the access semaphore and that the use of the vector of semaphores proclist implements a block/wake-up protocol. The above algorithm uses semaphores which only have two values. Request and release actually behave exactly like P and v except that they increment and decrement the variable avail. Such a generalization of the scmaphore principle can also be used directly with counting or general semaphores which, instead of taking just one of two values (1 and 0), can take any positive value. Request would then be equivalent to P(r) and release would be v(r) where r is a counting semaphore initialized to the number of resources available.

Other synchronization primitives

There are a number of other synchronization primitives which have been proposed. One possibility is a generalization of the mutexbegin and mutexend primitive where we have a number of different critical regions. Each region is allocated a 'gate', and instead of mutexbegin, a process performs a lock(gate), and instead of mutexend it executes an unlock(gate). A similar facility provided on the IBM 360/370 computers is the enqueue/dequeue commands which also allow queueing of processes entering and leaving critical regions.

PL/1 provides a variation on the block/wake-up theme. Rather than processes actually activating other processes a synchronization variable called an event (e) is defined (usually initialized to false). Possible operations are

wait(e)	block process until e is true
completion(e) = true	set e to true
completion(e) = false	set e to false .

Wait does not change the value of e, so repeated use of an event requires resetting its value to false after a wait.

Finally, we will consider a variation on the fork/join/quit approach. A new process is created by a call of the form

call p event(e) .

Such a child process is terminated by an exit statement which sets e to true. An exit statement is thus equivalent to a quit instruction and in the parent process a wait(e) is like a join.

Summary

In this chapter we have explored some of the notations which have been proposed for controlling parallel processes which, of necessity, share variables. The ideas have been developed mainly for use in multiprocessing operating systems. The same constructs can be used for developing parallel algorithms on multiprocessors. Implementing the constructs is more difficult in this context and we have to rely more heavily on hardware interlock mechanisms to prevent simultaneous write operations.

In a distributed processing system communication is usually much looser with processes communicating via messages. The synchronization primitives we have discussed in this chapter then become applicable at the operating system level where the message-passing protocols are implemented.

There are two more approaches to writing parallel programs which we have not yet covered. The first of these is the use of communicating sequential processes. This is the subject of the next chapter. The final possibility is to revise totally the style of programming by removing all assumed sequentiality from the notation. This involves adopting an alternative model of computing such as the data flow or functional approaches. We will defer discussion of this alternative until Part 4 where future computer architectures which actually use this approach are discussed.

Further reading

As we have mentioned, much of the work on synchronization primitives has been motivated by operating system design for multiprogrammed or multiprocess systems. Appropriate texts which discuss this application area are Ben-Ari (1982) and Holt (1983). The latter book contains much material which has been updated from Holt *et al.* (1978).

Chapter 11

Communicating Sequential Processes and Occam

In the last chapter we discussed how concurrent processes might interact using shared variables. We found that the synchronization problem was not easy. In this chapter we will examine an alternative approach to specifying the behaviour of concurrent processes. Processes are assumed to run sequentially. The synchronization is done in terms of communication channels.

The approach we will discuss is based on the ideas originally developed by Tony Hoare in the late 1970s. Inmos have taken Hoare's approach as the basis for their language occam. Occam is specifically designed to be used on transputers. We will attempt to introduce occam in parallel with the description of Hoare's model.

The primitive operations are input (represented by ?) and output (represented by !). An input process is represented by the statement

channel ? variable,

meaning that a value is received from the channel and placed in the variable. An output process is similar

channel ! expression.

The value of the expression is output along the channel. Processes may be named, as we will see later. In occam, processes communicate by naming channels not processes, whereas in the original specification of

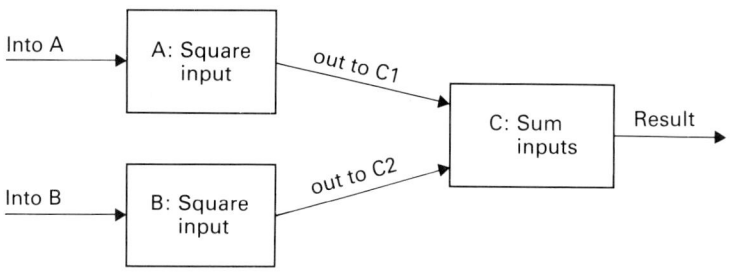

Fig. 11.1 Three processes to sum the squares of two numbers.

Communicating Sequential Processes and Occam

communicating sequential processes (CSP) given by Hoare the names of processes were used.

It is often convenient to draw simple diagrams to illustrate how processes are interacting. Consider three processes (as shown in Fig. 11.1). Processes A and B square their inputs and pass them on to process C which adds them together. Process A can be described in Hoare's CSP by two statements which must be executed sequentially. First, a value is received from the user

USER ? x.

Next, this value is squared and sent to the process C

c ! x * x .

Process B can be described in a similar manner (the semi-colon denotes sequential execution)

USER ? y ; c ! y * y .

Turning to process C this accepts two inputs which may arrive in any order. Therefore a parallel construct is required

A ? x ∥ B ? y .

The double vertical bar (∥) denotes parallel execution. The final stage is the outputting of the sum of these inputs to the user

USER ! x + y .

If we now use square brackets ([ ]) to group processes and add names to processes using a double colon notation (::) the whole system could be described by the following parallel command

[A :: USER?x ; c!x*x ∥ B :: USER?y ; c!y*y ∥ C :: [A?x ∥ B?y] ; USER!x+y] .

Note that the three processes A, B and C can theoretically be executed in parallel. In full CSP we would have to introduce variable declarations for x and y, but doing so would merely serve to clutter up the notation at the moment.

The occam descriptions of processes A and B are similar

A: VAR X :
        SEQ
          intoa ?x
          outtoc1 ! x * x

B: VAR X :
        SEQ
          intob ?x
          outtoc2 ! x * x .

Note that the variable x declared in each process is local to that process. The constructor SEQ causes all the statements following it and indented to be executed sequentially. Occam uses indentation to mark the start and end of blocks rather than the Pascal style convention of using terminating symbols like end. A basic difference is that whilst CSP uses process names in its input and output statements, occam uses named channels.

The process C can accept inputs from A and B in parallel so we need to introduce a parallel constructor

```
VAR x, y :
SEQ
  PAR
    outtoc1 ? x
    outtoc2 ? y
  result ! x + y
```

Here we have two unnamed processes inputting values from the channels outtoc1 and outtoc2 in parallel. When these have terminated the variables x and y are added together and the result output. Note how we have used indentation to show that the two parallel processes must be done before the output process.

These three processes could have been combined into one occam program. In the program we need to declare the channels as well

Communicating Sequential Processes and Occam 127

```
CHAN intoa, intob, outtoc1, outtoc2, result :
PAR
  VAR x :
  SEQ
    intoa   ? x
    outtoc1 ! x * x
  VAR x :
  SEQ
    intob   ? x
    outtoc2 ! x * x
  VAR x, y :
  SEQ
    PAR
      outtoc1 ? x
      outtoc2 ? y
    result ! x + y .
```

The two processes A and B were very similar so it would seem reasonable to expect that there would be some way of writing a parameterized sub-routine which could be used to describe both. Occam of course allows processes to be named and parameters used. If we did this for all three processes the above example would be rewritten as below

```
PROC square(CHAN in, out) =
  VAR x :
  SEQ
    in  ? x
    out ! x * x

PROC sum(CHAN in1, in2, out) =
  VAR x, y :
  SEQ
    PAR
      in1 ? x
      in2 ? y
    out ! x + y

CHAN intoa, intob, outtoc1, outtoc2, result :
PAR
  square(intoa, outtoc1)
  square(intob, outtoc2)
  sum(outtoc1, outtoc2, result) .
```

This program will only input one pair of values and produce one result. If we wanted the process to run continuously we would have to add some form of repetition. This is done in occam by using the WHILE constructor. This constructor works in a similar way to the SEQ and PAR constructs but clearly requires a condition to be associated with it. To make the squaring process an infinite process we would write

```
PROC squareforever(CHAN in, out) =
  WHILE TRUE
    VAR x :
    SEQ
      in  ? x
      out ! x * x .
```

To make it square only ten values for example, we would have to introduce some counting mechanism

```
PROC squareten(CHAN in, out) =
  VAR count :
  SEQ
    count := 0
    WHILE count < 10
      VAR x :
      PAR
        SEQ
          in  ? x
          out ! x * x
        count := count + 1 .
```

Note how we have allowed the incrementing of the count to take place in parallel with the actual squaring process.

Only two more basic constructions remain to be introduced — conditional processes and alternative processes. Both these constructs are concerned with making decisions depending upon what is happening at run-time. In Hoare's original notation these two constructs were combined into one construct — a list of guarded commands. A guard was either a boolean expression which returns a value true or false, or an input construct which failed when there was no input. A typical guarded command using boolean expressions as guards might be

$[x >= y \rightarrow m := x \square y >= x \rightarrow m := y]$.

Communicating Sequential Processes and Occam 129

The semantics of this construct were that you should execute one of the commands whose guard does not fail. Therefore in the example given, if x>y then the first command (m:=y) will be executed. If x<y then the second command (m:=y) will be executed. If x=y then either of the two commands may be executed non-deterministically. In this case it wouldn't matter which. In occam this would be expressed as a conditional construct

```
IF
  x >= y
    m := x
  x <= y
    m := y .
```

The semantics of this construct are slightly different. In occam it is specified that the first component (or guarded expression) for which the expression (guard) is true is the one evaluated. Therefore if $x = y$ the first option would be selected. One advantage of this semantic interpretation is that it allows the use of a default case at the end. By using a guard TRUE we can ensure that one process is always executed.

To illustrate the other form of guarded expression we will return to our initial sum of squares example. In Hoare's CSP notation the infinite squaring process would have been written

$*[\,x : \text{integer}; \text{in} ? x \rightarrow \text{out} ! x * x\,].$

The asterisk indicates repetition and we have declared the variable x to be of type integer. The original specification of occam is unclear on how types are dealt with. This repetitive process will terminate when the guard 'in ? x' fails because there is no input. The squaring process could have been written to accept inputs from two alternative channels

$*[\,x : \text{integer}; \text{in1} ? x \;\rightarrow\; \text{out} ! x * x$
$\square\, x : \text{integer}; \text{in2} ? x \;\rightarrow\; \text{out} ! x * x\,].$

Here the process accepts an input value on either channel in1 or channel in2. This is the usual use of the ALT construct in occam

```
WHILE TRUE
  VAR X :
  ALT
    in1 ? x
      out ! x * x
    in2 ? x
      out ! x * x .
```

The ALT construct retains the non-deterministic semantics of arbitrarily selecting a process if two guards evaluate to true.

As well as allowing input processes to act as guards alone, the ALT construct allows them to be combined with boolean expressions. Suppose we wished to limit the number of values accepted from each channel to be within two of the other then we could write something like the following occam process

```
PROC squareevenly(CHAN in1, in2, out) :
VAR count :
SEQ
  count := 0
  WHILE TRUE
    VAR x :
    ALT
      count <= 2 & in1 ? x
        PAR
          out ! x * x
          count := count + 1
      count >= -2 & in2 ? x
        PAR
          out ! x * x
          count := count - 1 .
```

The first process increments count, but it is never allowed to become greater than two, so it can never input more than two values more than the second input process which decrements the count.

We can use the expressions in guards to reintroduce non-determinism into our simple maximum function as occam allows a SKIP function in ALT constructs which is always ready

```
ALT
  x <= y & SKIP
    m := y
  x >= y & SKIP
    m := x .
```

Having introduced briefly both occam and the basic idea of CSP we will now present some example processes in both CSP and occam. To do so we will need to introduce some additional notation in passing. Firstly, let us write a process x which copies characters from a channel west to a channel east replacing pairs of asterisks ('**') by a single asterisk ('*'). For convenience we assume that the final character is not an asterisk. In Hoare's CSP we would write a repetitive program using guarded commands

```
*[ c : character; west ? c →
        [ c <> '*' → east ! c
        ▯ c =  '*' →west ? c ;
                [ c <> '*' → east ! '*' ; east ! c
                ▯ c =  '*' → east ! '*'
                ]
        ]
]
```

In occam the same process could be written using the WHILE, ALT and IF constructs

```
PROC compress(CHAN west, east) =
    VAR c :
    WHILE TRUE
        ALT
            west ? c
                IF
                    c <> '*'
                        east ! c
                    c =  '*'
                        SEQ
                            west ? c
                            IF
                                c <> '*'
                                    SEQ
                                        east ! '*'
                                        east ! c
                                c = '*'
                                    east ! '*' .
```

Often a number of processes are all behaving in a similar fashion. One such situation is illustrated by a factorial program which uses a series of processes to perform the calculation. This is illustrated in Fig. 11.2. Both CSP and occam give us shorthand ways of replicating similar processes. First of all, in CSP we name an array of processes

fac(i : 1..limit)

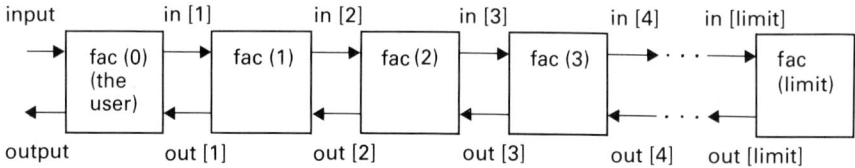

Fig. 11.2 A vector of processes to calculate the factorial of a number.

The parameter i indicates which of the processes we are referring to. We clearly have to specify how many we want and this is indicated by the range expression 1..limit. The complete description of the factorial program is given below. Note how CSP names processes rather than channels. The process USER is used to represent the interaction with the outside world. Each process receives a value, decrements it and sends it on to the next process in line. When a value is received back, it is multiplied by the first value received and the result sent on back to the initiating process

```
[ fac(i:1..limit) : :
       *[ n : integer; fac(i − 1) ? n →
              [ n = 0 → fac(i − 1) ! 1
              ☐ n > 0 → fac(i+1) ! n − 1;
                     r : integer;
                     fac(i + 1) ? r;
                     fac(i − 1) ! (n ∗ r)
              ]
       ]
|| fac(0) : : USER .
]
```

In occam the above program would be written using the replicator construct FOR. We also need to specify a vector of channels and this is done by adding a count after the name of the channel

```
CHAN out[limit], in[limit], input, output :
PAR
  VAR x :
  SEQ
    input ? x
    out[1] ! x
    in[1] ? x
    output ! x
  PAR i = [1 FOR limit]
    VAR n :
    SEQ
      in[i] ? n
      IF
        n = 0
          out[1] ! 1
        n > 0
          VAR r :
          SEQ
            in[i+1] ! n − 1
            out[i+1] ? r
            out[i] ! n ∗ r .
```

Another application of a vector of processes is a sorting vector. Each process receives a value from its predecessor. If this is the first value received it is retained by the process. If it is an end of input value then it is propagated on. Otherwise the process retains the smaller of the value it holds or the value received. Eventually one processor will receive an end of input value but will not be holding a value. This processor simply echoes the end of input value back to its predecessor. When a process receives a value from its successor it outputs its own value to its predecessor followed by all the values received from its successor. The output from the first process is the values in ascending order followed by the end of input value. Some example stages in this process are illustrated in Fig. 11.3. We will use 0 as the end of input value. Let us now write this program in both CSP and occam. This program is given in CSP in Fig. 11.4 and in occam in Fig. 11.5.

134   Chapter 11

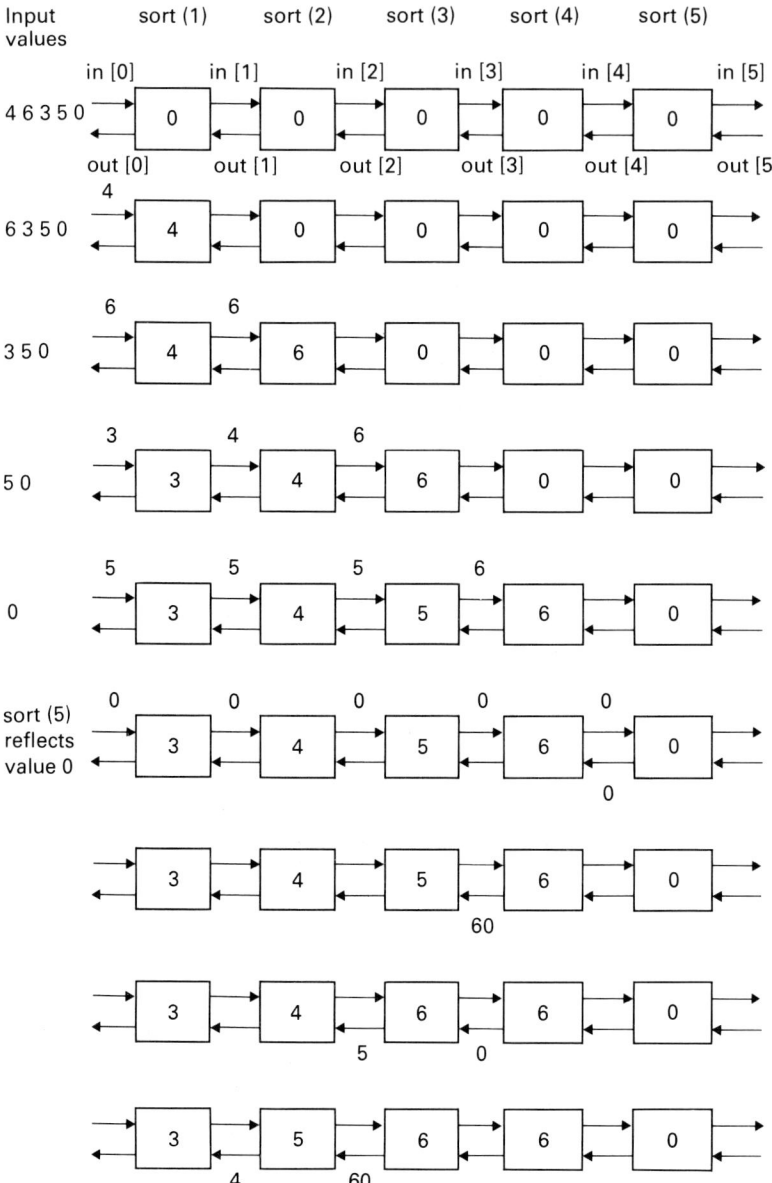

Fig. 11.3 Stages in the execution of a sorting vector.

```
[sort(i : 1..limit) : :
  held : integer;
  sort(i−1) ? held;
  [ held = 0 →
        sort(i−1) ! 0
  □ held <> 0 →
        *[ received : integer;
           sort(i−1) ? received →
               [ received = 0 →
                     sort(i+1) ! 0
               □ received > 0 and received < held →
                     sort(i+1) ! held;
                     held := received
               □ received >= held →
                     sort(i+1) ! received
               ]
           □ sort(i+1) ? received →
               [ received = 0 →
                     sort(i−1) ! held;
                     sort(i−1) ! 0
               □ received <> 0 →
                     sort(i−1) ! held;
                     held := received
               ]
        ]
  ]
]
].
```

Fig. 11.4 The sorting program in CSP.

Summary and further reading

In this chapter we have introduced an alternative model of computation, namely that of co-operating sequential processes (CSP). We have also seen how it is possible to develop a programming language based on that model. In an earlier chapter we saw how a computer, the transputer, could be designed to implement such a language. Tony Hoare's original paper introducing his version of the CSP model was published in 1978 (Hoare, 1978). It is this notation we have chosen to use. Since the publication of that paper, a lot of work has been done using that model. In 1985 Hoare

```
CHAN in[limit], out[limit] :
VAR held :
SEQ i = [1 FOR limit]
  in[i−1] ? held
  IF
    held = 0
       out[i−1] ! 0
    held <> 0
       VAR received
         WHILE TRUE
           ALT
             in[i−1] ? received
               IF
                 received = 0
                    in[i] ! 0
                 received < held
                    SEQ
                      in[i] ! held
                      held := received
                 received >= held
                    in[i] ! received
             in[i] ? received
               IF
                 received = 0
                    SEQ
                      out[i−1] ! held
                      in[i−1] ! 0
                 received <> 0
                    SEQ
                      in[i−1] ! held
                      held := received .
```

Fig. 11.5 The sorting process in occam.

published a book which provides an excellent discussion of the whole subject, together with a short but useful list of further references (Hoare, 1978).

Inmos have produced a programming manual for occam which is published by Prentice-Hall (Inmos, 1984). Unfortunately this is little more than an expensive version of the slim guide which was given free with the early evaluation kits and contains only very short examples of program fragments (most even shorter than the ones included in this chapter). A much better introduction is a report written by Geraint Jones of the Programming Research Group at Oxford University. This is going to be published as a book, by Prentice-Hall, in the near future (Jones, 1987).

Part 4

Future Computer Architectures

In the preceding three parts of this book we have essentially been discussing the design and use of existing distributed and parallel processing systems. Many of these systems may form the basis of what the Japanese (amongst others) have chosen to term the fifth or new generation of computers currently being developed around the world. Many researchers believe, though, that in order to achieve a significant breakthrough in computer design we have to re-examine the fundamental model of computation represented by the stored program computer we are all used to. In this part we will present three approaches which adopt different views of the way in which computations are done. For each approach we present some ideas on how computers can be built to implement the new model. All the architectures include some parallelism. They are also distributed computers in the sense that the program and data are distributed throughout the machine.

Chapter 12

Data Flow Computing

So far in our discussion of parallel computing we have concentrated on ways of introducing parallelism into essentially sequential models. An alternative approach is to assume that everything is parallel unless it has to be sequential. This is the principle behind the data flow approach.

The data flow model of computing attempts to get round the problems encountered in introducing parallelism into the traditional control flow model by looking at the process of computation from a different viewpoint.

If we consider the five types of dependency introduced in Chapter 8 then the only dependency which could never be removed is flow dependency (a value had to be produced before it could be used). In essence a **data flow program** is one in which the order of operations is determined solely by the availability of resources and the flow dependencies.

Let us illustrate this idea by means of a simple example. The following program is designed to calculate the roots of a quadratic equation (assuming they exist) using a Pascal-like notation

```
begin
input(a, b, c);
a := 2 * a;
c := b ↑ 2 − 2 * a * c;
c := sqrt(c);
c := c / a;
b := −b / a;
a := b + c;
b := b − c;
output(a, b)
end .
```

To extract the parallelism using **fork** and **join** constructs we would have to write a program similar to the one below

141

142 Chapter 12

```
begin   input(a, b, c);
        a := 2 * a;
        c := b ↑ 2 − 2 * a * c;
        fork L1;
        c := sqrt(c);
        c := c / a;
        join;
        fork L2;
        a := b + c;
        join;
        output(a, b);
        exit;
L1:     b := b / a;
        quit;
L2:     b := b − c;
        quit;
end .
```

Expressing the program in terms of communicating sequential processors we would get the following program using an occam-like notation

```
PAR
   SEQ
      input ? a, b, c
      totwo ! b
      a := 2 * a
      totwo ! a
      c := b ↑ 2 − * a * c
      c := sqrt(c)
      totwo ! c
      toone ? b
      a := b + c
      toone ? c
      output ! a, c
   SEQ
      totwo ? b
      totwo ? a
      b := −b / a
      toone ? b
      totwo ? c
      c := b − c
      toone ! d .
```

Data Flow Computing

Neither version is particularly easy to read. Using simply flow dependency we get the graph shown in Fig. 12.1. The basis behind data flow is to take this one step further and express the dependencies not between statements (which are fairly arbitrary units anyway), but between operations. A typical data flow graph for the example program is given in Fig. 12.2.

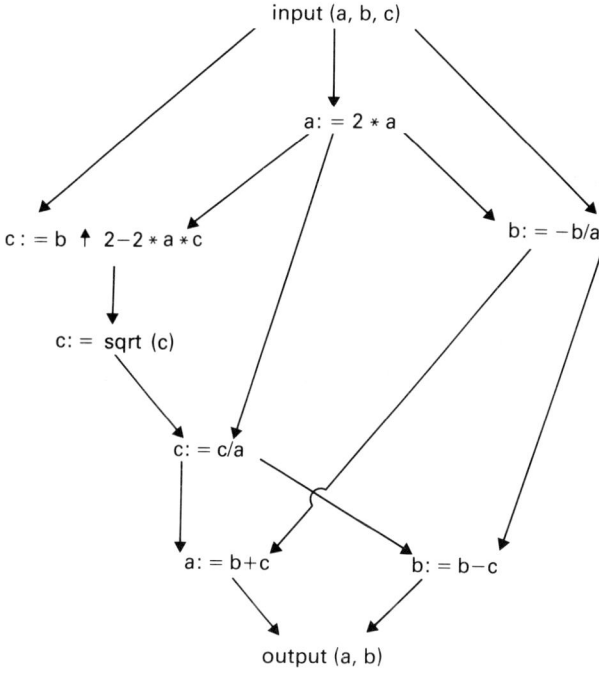

Fig. 12.1 Flow dependencies for the quadratic roots program (at statement level).

A data flow notation only requires five primitives (see Fig. 12.3). Execution is expressed in terms of nodes **firing** when sufficient inputs are present. In pictorial terms, data items are viewed as **tokens** flowing along the arcs connecting the nodes. A node fires by absorbing the tokens on its input arcs and placing the appropriate tokens on its output arcs. The gate node places a token on its output arc only if its control input is of the correct value. The merge or union node fires when either of its input arcs contains a token. If both contain a token at the same time it is undefined as to which is placed on the output arc first. The model of computing is in fact

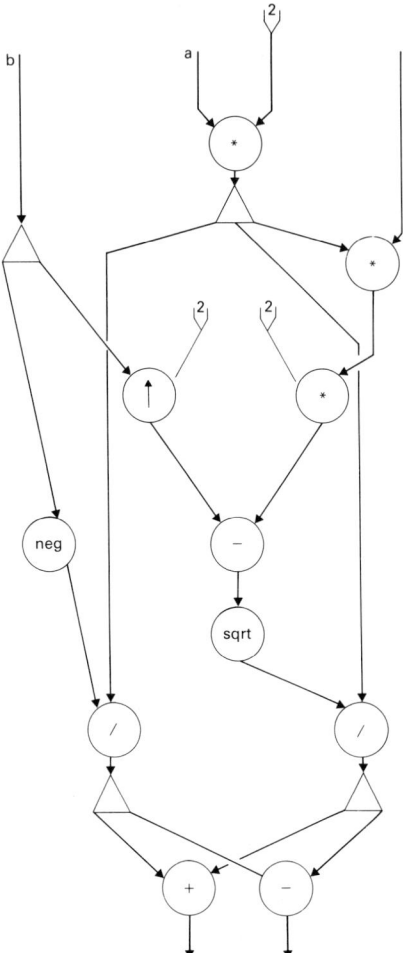

Fig. 12.2 Operation level data dependencies for the quadratic roots program.

made easier if we only ever place one value on an output arc. Repetition then has to be implemented in terms of recursion, but this is not difficult.

A program represents a set of possible computations. Depending upon the values of the input data, only one computation will be carried out. A **data flow computation** can be defined as one in which operations are executed in an order determined by the data interdependencies and the availability of resources. It is convenient for the moment to ignore the question of resource availability.

Data Flow Computing

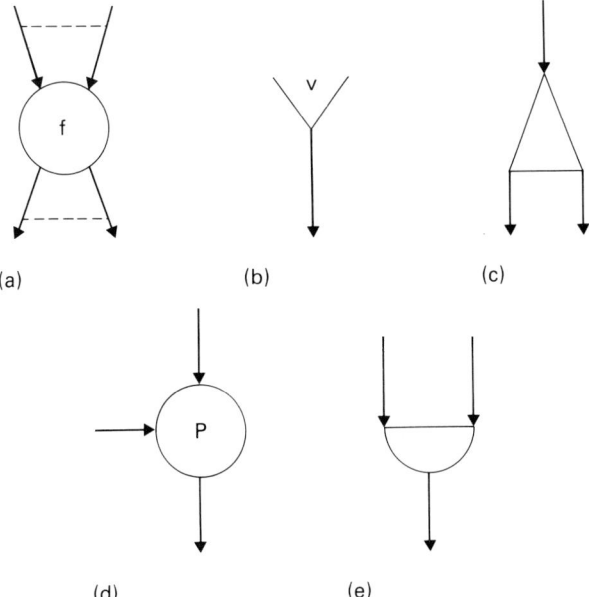

Fig. 12.3 Five primitive data flow nodes. (a) Primitive function; (b) Constant generator; (c) Copy node; (d) Gate node (input is passed only if control matches predicate P); (e) Non-deterministic merge node (first input to arrive is passed on).

It is possible to regard the data flow approach as a way of expressing parallel computation which can be used with any multiprocessor architecture. However, it is so radically different from the conventional approach that special architectures have been proposed which implement data flow programs directly. These architectures need some way of dynamically connecting processors. Each processor is envisaged as executing the function specified by an individual node. Outputs are produced and these outputs are paired up as inputs for subsequent operations.

Three basic types of architectures for implementing data flow programs can be identified.
(1) Static Architecture. This type is not really very interesting, since a truly static architecture can evaluate only one program graph. Possibly the only interesting static architecture would be one which could evaluate the program which could run any program (i.e. the interpreter). In this case, all the complexity of executing a data flow program would be transferred away from the architecture design to the

compilation stage. This may be an acceptable strategy although it is difficult to see how it would be decided what form the machine architecture should take.

(2) Reconfigurable Static Architecture. This means a machine (consisting of a number of processors) where the logical interconnections between the processors are made when the program is loaded. This implies that decisions about what connections are needed are made by the compiler and/or the loader and remain fixed throughout execution. This approach would seem to suggest that

(a) most possible physical connections must exist, and

(b) the number of processors available must be in excess of the minimum necessary, since it is difficult to see how optimal reuse of processors is possible with fixed links.

(3) Dynamic Architecture. This architecture is by far the most interesting, since it is the only type which allows programs to be evaluated dynamically. The main feature of a dynamic architecture is that the logical connections between processors can be changed during the execution of a program.

A generalized block diagram of a dynamic data flow architecture is given in Fig. 12.4. One possible source of variation in this design is in the construction of the communication network. When modern program design techniques are used, the resulting programs tend to have a hierarchical structure. This is also true of data flow programs, where initially abstract/complex operations at nodes can be refined by graphs (programs) constructed of simpler nodes (operations).

Drawing a diagram of the logical structure would yield a tree. Control flows from the roots to the leaves and results flow back from the leaves to the roots. This rather simplified view would seem to suggest that the logical connections between processors in a data flow machine should be representable as a tree.

An obvious architecture would seem to be a physical representation of the logical tree structure. A moment's thought, however, should show that such an architecture would require many more processors than the minimum number required for any particular computation, and that it would be difficult (if not impossible) to ensure that all possible parallelism would be exploited. After all, the tree structure would be static and we have argued that we need a dynamic architecture. A partially dynamic tree architecture designed to execute Lisp programs has been designed by a team working at Utah. A block diagram of this proposal is given in Fig. 12.5.

Data Flow Computing 147

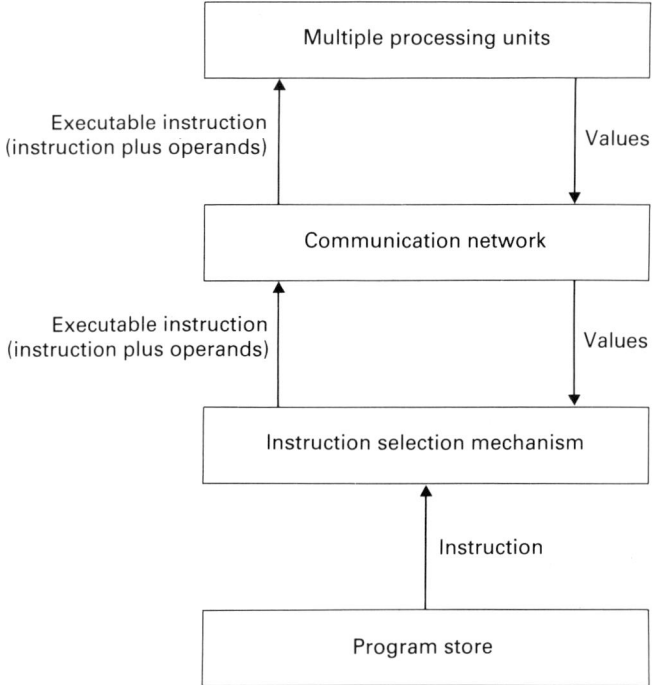

Fig. 12.4 Generalized block diagram of a data flow processor.

An alternative to the simple tree design is to make the network more general. A design such as CalTech's Hypercube could be used, but since we are talking about relatively small amounts of computation being carried out at each node, even with this design the overhead of communicating via a number of processors could soon become unacceptable.

One design which allows any processor to communicate with any other is the Manchester data flow machine which uses a ring structure with all communication passing through a switch. A single ring is shown in Fig. 12.6. In this design there are a number of processors, each producing results. These are returned to a memory/control unit which collects together the results required by subsequent operations and generates new tasks (operations and required inputs) which are passed around the ring. Results will be produced by the processing units at different rates at different stages of execution, depending upon the number and complexity of the operations currently being performed. At certain times results may be produced faster than the matching store can process them. The result queue is a way of temporarily storing such results.

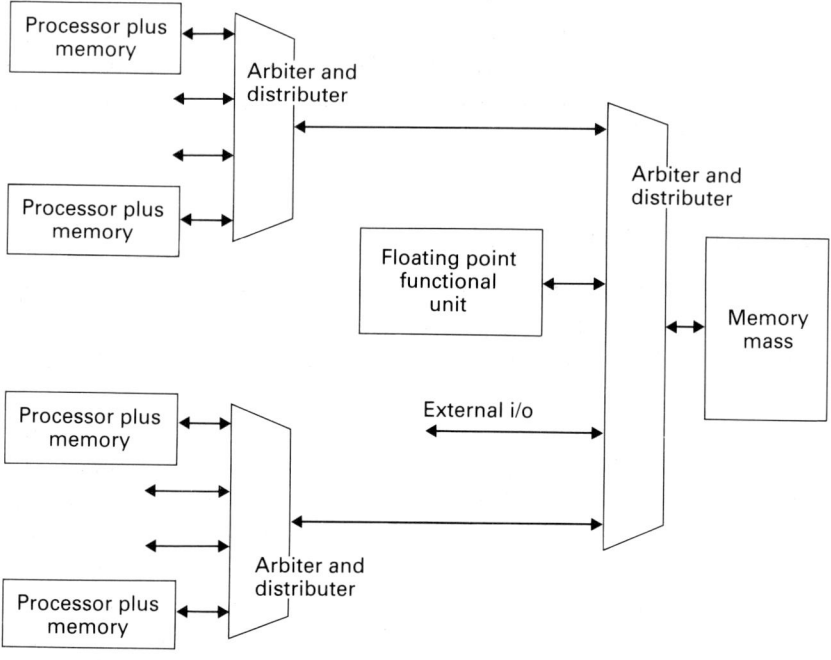

Fig. 12.5 A Lisp machine based on a tree architecture.

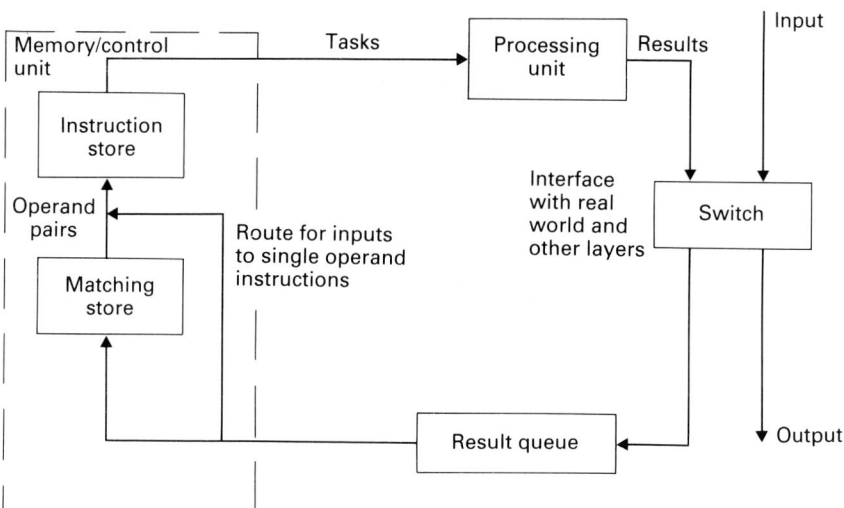

Fig. 12.6 The Manchester data flow machine.

A number of rings may be connected together in parallel layers with a switch allowing communication between the rings. In such an architecture the control function may be distributed between the different layers, but we still have a logical cyclic construction with a separation of the control and execution tasks.

Summary and further reading

We have introduced briefly the data flow approach as an alternative to the conventional von Neumann model of computing. We have also outlined briefly two possible approaches to implementing this approach directly in hardware.

There are three main groups working on data flow. In Britain the Manchester group headed by John Gurd have succeeded in producing a simple working prototype. The first section of Chambers *et al.* (1984) (Chapters 1–4) was written by them and provides a reasonable introduction to their data flow approach. For a more recent update on their achievements so far, the reader should refer to Gurd *et al.* (1985).

The other two main groups are both at MIT. One is headed by Jack Dennis (Dennis, 1980) and the other by Arvind (Arvind & Kathail, 1981). For an overall introduction to data flow without any bias to a particular hardware approach the reader is referred to Sharp (1985). In 1982 Phil Treleaven and some colleagues published a review of actual system which had been proposed (Treleaven *et al.* 1982). Also in 1982 the IEEE devoted a special issue of their Computer magazine to data flow systems (IEEE, 1982). Phil Treleaven also contributed Section 1 of Tiberghien (1984). This section, as well as introducing data flow computers, discusses various other approaches including reduction machines (which are discussed in the next chapter of this book). For those interested in the future of computer architecture the whole book is worth a look.

The Utah Lisp machine which was mentioned briefly is described in more detail in Keller *et al.* (1979).

Chapter 13

The Functional Approach

In the previous chapter we presented the data flow appraoch of computing using a graphical model. This approach uses the availability of data to drive the execution of a program. The subject of this chapter is the functional programming approach to computing. We will start by defining a functional version of the data flow model.

A program defines a mapping from an input domain to an output range. Our earlier discussion assumed the existence of operations which perform such mappings, albeit at a lower level. To formalize the data flow model we have to make the concept of an operation more explicit. In a theoretical sense it is pleasing to make the basis of a model as simple and as primitive as possible. To this end we shall follow convention and define a basic boolean domain for our operations

$$B = \{ \text{TRUE, FALSE} \} .$$

We could equally well have defined a binary domain

$$B_i = \{ 0, 1 \} ,$$

but initially the logical representation seems to add clarity. Later we shall refer to a basic binary domain, and with this in mind we note the equivalence $B \equiv B_i$.

Conventional logic tells us that the only primitive operation we require is NOR (or NAND).

The primitive operation: nor

This operation is defined by a function $B \times B \rightarrow B$ as follows

$$\text{nor} = [\, a : \text{TRUE}, b : B \quad] \text{FALSE} ,$$
$$\text{nor} = [\, a : \text{FALSE}, b : \text{FALSE}] \text{TRUE} ,$$
$$\text{nor} = [\, a : \text{FALSE}, b : \text{TRUE} \,] \text{FALSE} .$$

We shall term this method of defining functions as 'definition by cases'. The method of 'definition by cases' is the main definitional mechanism provided in this functional data flow model. It may be summarized as shown below

< name of function > = [< parameter > : < domain >] < value (or
     (repeated for each of   expression
     parameters)   giving value
             in this case)>

A constant generator

The only other basic operation necessary is a constant generator. We shall take as primitive a true generator. This operation requires no input parameter so we introduce the null set {NULL} as a possible domain. True is defined by a function NULL → TRUE as below

true = [ ] TRUE .

A false generator could be defined in two ways

Either false = [ ] FALSE,
or false = [ ] nor(true, true) .

A copy operation

In combinational logic this operation is usually assumed and it is not essential if we are allowed to specify the format of the input in a suitable manner (i.e. by repeating input values to avoid copying). Copy is defined by a function B → B × B as below

copy = [a : B] (a, a) .

Complex operations

Our mechanism for constructing operations by defining cases allows us to construct many operations. It is useful to be able to refer to groups of operations by name (i.e. assign names to definitions). In the above definition of nor, the name nor was assigned to three expressions which define what the name nor means when associated with various parameters. If we then allow an operation to be built up out of any named operations, including itself, we are in a position to define any operation which we might require. It is possible to build up a high-level language from these primitive operations. It is important to realize that the method of definition by cases is a tool to build programs; in any computation only one case will be executed.

Since all the primitive operations are functional, and we can only define operations by means of composition of operations and other functions (as outlined above) we can say that: any operation is such that its output(s) are a function of its input(s).

The functional model presented does not depend upon the arrival of data values to drive the execution. It is perfectly possible to envisage a system which is controlled by requests for data.

Consider the quadratic roots program again. We require the outputs a and b. Thus the two statements 'a := b + c' and 'b := b − c' must be evaluated. In order to do so we need to know the values of b and c. (Note that we originally wanted the final value of b referred to on the left hand side of the statement; we now require the penultimate value referred to on the right hand side of the assignment.) Requests for these values can be passed back to the statements which generate them

'c := c/a' and 'b := − b/a'.

Eventually, requests can be passed back until the input values are requested. This view of the evaluation process is known as the **demand-driven** approach, since execution is controlled by the demands (requests) for data. The term **lazy evaluation** is also used sometimes, since only values which are actually needed are evaluated, and then only when they are needed and not before. A request for a data value can in fact be interpreted as a request for a method of calculating that value. The value may or may not be used later. Evaluation is only carried out when absolutely necessary — hence the use of the term 'lazy'.

This functional model is built upon the idea of combining functions in certain ways. The programming language Lisp is often regarded as a classic example of this approach to computing, and in many ways the model we have presented may be seen as similar. Implicit in this model, however, is the concept of functions being applied to data items and to the results of functions. The pure functional approach of combining only functions is best reflected in Backus' FP. An FP system consists of

(1) A set of **objects.** These are the basic values manipulated by the system.
(2) A set of **functions** to map objects to objects. Examples of typical functions are selector functions (to select an element of a sequence), list reversal and the usual arithmetic functions.
(3) A single operation — **application.**
(4) A set of **functional forms** which are used to combine existing functions or objects to form new functions.
(5) A set of **definitions,** which give names to functions.

The Functional Approach

The only operation in an FP system is **application.** The power of an FP system comes from its ability to combine functions to form new functions. Four possible functional forms are

(1) **Composition** $(f \circ g){:}x = f{:}(g{:}x)$. The composition of functions f and g applied to an object x is the same as the function f applied to the result of applying g to x.

(2) **Construction** $[f1, \ldots, fn]{:}x = <f1{:}x, \ldots, fn{:}x>$. The list of functions f1 to fn applied to x is the list of results obtained by applying each f to x.

(3) **Condition** $(p \rightarrow f;g){:}x = $ if $(p{:}x)$ is true then $f{:}x$; if $(p{:}x)$ is false then $g{:}x$; otherwise undefined. Either f or g is applied to x depending on whether p applied to x yields true or false.

(4) **Constant** $\bar{x}{:}y = x$, where x is an object.

Using these functional forms we can express the factorial function '!' as

$$eq0 \rightarrow \bar{1}; \times [id, !\circ sub1].$$

The functions eq0 and sub1 are defined

$$eq0 = eq \circ [id, \bar{0}]$$
$$sub1 = - \circ [id, \bar{1}]$$

(id is the identity function, × multiplication, − subtraction and eq the equality operation).

The definition of eq0 may be read as
apply the identity operation and the 0 constant function
giving a list of two objects — the value and zero;
test for equality.

The definition of sub1 may be read as
apply the identity operation and the 1 constant function
giving a list of two objects — the value and 1;
perform a subtraction.

The definition of factorial may thus be read as
apply the test 'if equals 0';
if the answer is true then apply the 1 constant function (return the value 1);
otherwise (not equal to zero) multiply the pair of values resulting from:
applying the identity function and applying the factorial to the value less 1.

The important characteristic of FP to note is that nowhere in the program (definition of factorial) is there any mention of the value being manipulated. In other words, the characteristics of the data (type, etc.)

have been separated totally from the description of the actions to be performed.

Thus the concepts of variables and assignments which are characteristic of the control flow model of computing have been totally eliminated.

Having introduced the functional model of computing we shall now examine briefly two methods which have been proposed for implementing functional programs in hardware. Both are based on the concept of reduction.

In simple terms, reduction means replacing part of the original source code by its meaning. For example, if one expression in the program is '2 * 3' then it can be reduced to '6'.

This implies that reduction takes place by string replacement. This type of reduction is called 'string reduction'. There is an alternative approach which uses a graphical representation of the code and pointers are manipulated rather than code being copied. This is known as 'graph reduction'.

The first machine design we will consider is one which uses string reduction. It is a tree-based design developed by Gyula Mago of Chapel Hill, North Carolina. The design is based on using large numbers of relatively simple components and is intended to be ideal for VLSI. The basic interconnection of cells is shown in Fig. 13.1. The horizontal connections between the leaves can, according to Mago, be omitted without impairing the machine's capabilities.

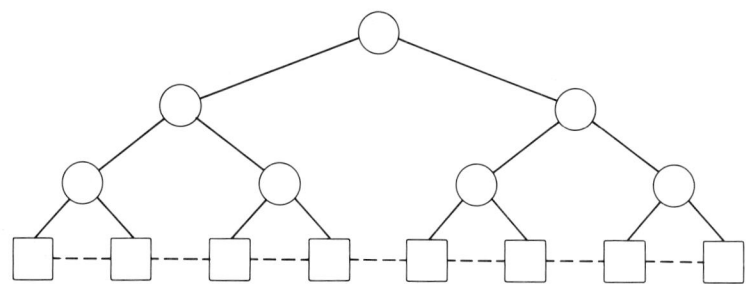

Fig. 13.1 Basic tree structure of Mago's machine.

Figure 13.2 shows how the tree structure can be laid out on a chip using VLSI. This design is easily extensible.

The program to be evaluated is an FFP program and is placed directly into the leaf cells. This implies that either the tree must be large enough to

The Functional Approach

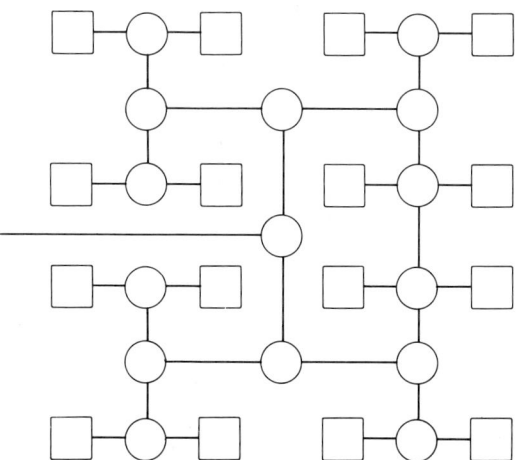

Fig. 13.2 VLSI layout of a binary tree structure.

contain the whole program, or that only parts of the program are evaluated at once. An example is given in Fig. 13.3. The innermost applications are grouped together as reducible applications (RAs). Each RA is contained within a separate tree and can be reduced independently, giving a new set

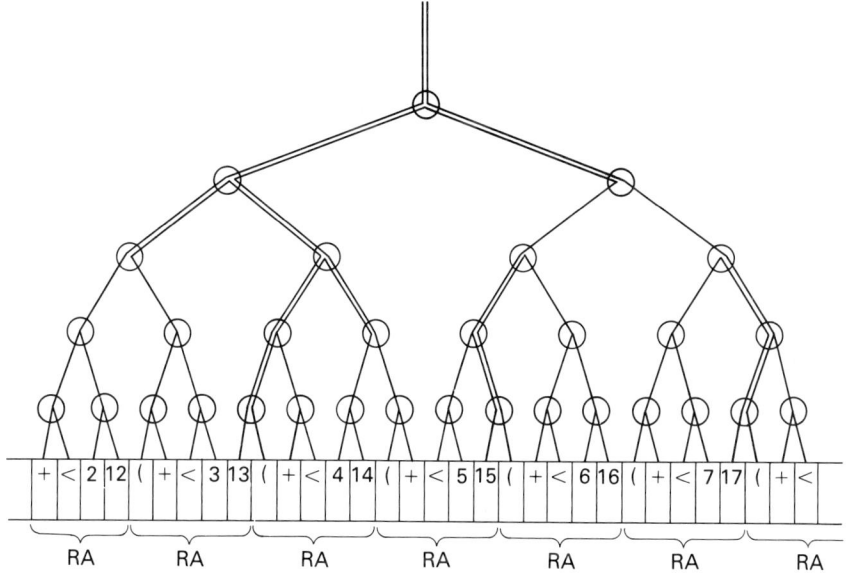

Fig. 13.3 An FFP program in Mago's tree machine.

```
Initial expression :(⟨AA,+⟩ : ⟨1,11⟩,⟨2,12⟩,⟨3,13⟩,⟨4,14⟩ )
AA means to Apply to All
Step 1 — remove redundant closing⟩
         and rewrite ( with ⟨
                    :⟨⟨AA,+ :⟨1,11 ,⟨2,12 ,⟨3,13 ,⟨4,14 )
Step 2 — rewrite ⟨ with (
                    :⟨(AA,+ :⟨1,11 ,⟨2,12 ,⟨3,13 ,⟨4,14 )
Step 3 — erase AA and mark '+'
                    :⟨( + :⟨1,11 ,⟨2,12 ,⟨3,13 ,⟨4, 14 )
Step 4 — erase leftmost symbol and
         insert the string (+ : on left
         of <      :⟨(+ :⟨1,11 (+ :⟨2,12 (+ :⟨3,13 (+ :⟨4,14 )
Step 5 — perform addition
                    : ⟨( 12, 14, 16, 18 )
```

Fig. 13.4 Stages in the reduction process for Apply to All.

of leaves which are grouped into RAs. The process is then repeated until eventually only one RA remains which reduces to the result required. Figure 13.4 shows some example steps.

One problem of the string reduction approach used here is the need to re-evaluate common sub-expressions. A graph reduction approach avoids this problem. One design which uses graph reduction is the Alice design proposed by Darlington and Reeve of Imperial College, London.

Let us first clarify the difference between graph reduction and string reduction. Consider the definition below

a = (b+c)*(b−c) .

In string reduction a request for the value of a would result in a copy of the definition (b+c)*(b−c) being taken. Then a value of b would be requested, giving say

(4+c)*(b−c) .

Evaluation would proceed with the string being rewritten through the following steps

(4+2)*(b−c)
  6*(b−c)
  6*(4−c)
  6*(4−2)
     6*2
      12 .

The two brackets could be evaluated in parallel but the values of b and c would be copied twice.

If the same problem were to be evaluated using graph reduction, the point at which a was requested would be given a pointer to the definition.

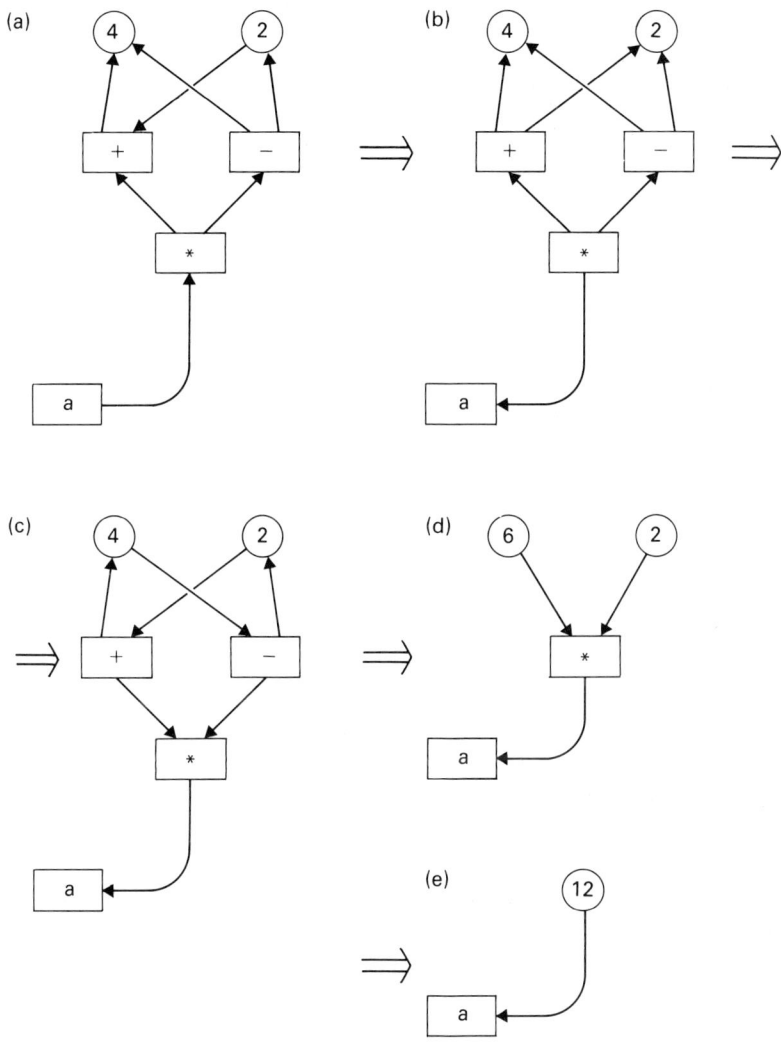

Fig. 13.5 Stages in a graph reduction. (a) Initial graph; (b) A request for 'a' reverses the link between 'a' and its definition; (c) Eventually all the arcs are reversed; (d) The first stage of the evaluation; (e) The result is produced.

This arc would be traversed (and reversed to allow for a value to be returned). Eventually all the arcs would have been traversed and reversed. Values would then be returned down the arcs, eventually arriving back at the point of the original request. This process is illustrated in Fig. 13.5.

The point to note is that if the definition of b had itself been a complex expression, in the string reduction example it would have been evaluated twice, whereas in the graph reduction example it would only need to be evaluated once.

Turning now to the Alice machine, operations (nodes in the graph) are represented by packets. The above example would be represented by the packets shown in Fig. 13.6. Evaluation proceeds by a number of processors each selecting packets which are ready to be evaluated (or reduced), performing the appropriate operations and returning the packets to a pool. The actual method for allowing processors (packet rewriting agents) to communicate has taken various forms during the history of the Alice project. It has been influenced more by the hardware available than the logical design. The latest architecture proposal is illustrated in Fig. 13.7.

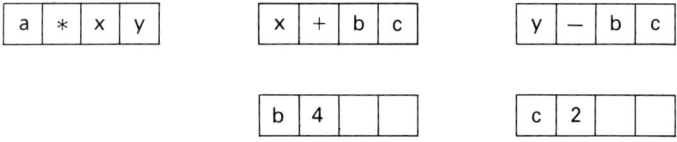

Fig. 13.6 Alice packets to represent the computation.

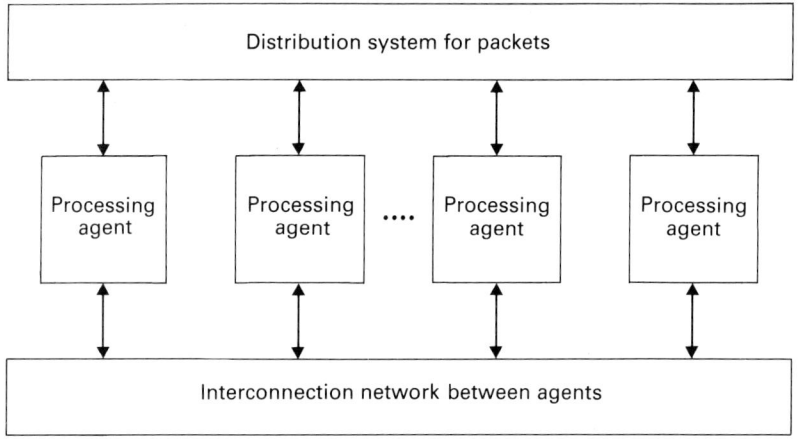

Fig. 13.7 A possible architecture for Alice.

Summary

In this chapter we have examined another approach to computing which assumes parallelism and only introduces sequentiality when necessary. We started by introducing the functional approach as a theoretical model for the data flow approach. This is perhaps rather misleading as the functional approach has been around for much longer. It might be regarded as the original approach to computation used by mathematicians before computers were invented. Some people might consider it ironic that as we reach the limits of what can be achieved in terms of performance by what has become the traditional approach to computing, we are now turning back to the mathematicians' theoretical view.

The reason for this renewed interest in what was once considered a purely academic approach is that we are now able to see possible ways of implementing this approach efficiently. In this chapter we have only introduced briefly two possible machine architectures which seem to be heading towards the ultimate in decentralized control of computation. There are a number of other possible approaches which we do not have time to go into now.

Further reading

The development of a functional approach to the data flow model is described in more detail in Sharp (1985). The first description of Backus' FP and FFP was given in Backus' Turing Award Lecture (Backus, 1978). Descriptions of the two architectures are given in Mago (1980) and Darlington & Reeve (1981). A review of architectures for implementing functional languages was published by Vegdahl (Vegdahl, 1984).

A good general introduction to functional programming is to be found in Glaser *et al.* (1984).

Chapter 14

The Connection Machine

Parallel computers can be designed as general purpose machines which should be able to increase the throughput for virtually any application. Most multiprocessors fall into this category. The data flow and functional approaches discussed in the previous chapters are also believed to be applicable to a wide range of problems. An alternative approach (which the designers of array processors have taken) is to choose an application area which is clearly suited to parallel processing and design a machine which will exploit the type of parallelism common in that application. The application area chosen is usually large scale numerical computation. Another area where a lot of computation can be done in parallel is in artificial intelligence, particularly in the use of semantic networks. It was for this application that the connection machine was originally designed. It turns out, however, that the resulting machine is generally applicable to a wider range of problems.

The concept behind the connection machine was the idea that a semantic network could be most rapidly manipulated if each data node in the network had a dedicated processor. Because of the application area there is a large potential for parallel computation at each node, so this sort of design would not be excessively wasteful of resources — assuming our node processors were not too expensive. We are talking about semantic networks with millions of nodes so clearly our processors have to be small and cheap — we will come to their actual design in a moment. First though, a word about the connections in the network. The ideal design would be for the network to be hardwired for any particular application (network). Only in exceptional circumstances is this likely to be acceptable. Therefore we need some form of switching network. The connection machine therefore, like all the other parallel processors suggested, has two components — processing elements and a communication network. We will now look at each of these in more detail and outline how it is suggested that such a machine could be programmed.

The cells

Figure 14.1 shows the basic structure of a cell. It consists of some memory, a small processor and a communicator. The rule table is identical for all cells and can thus be shared between adjacent cells on a chip. Its purpose is to tell the cell how to behave when it receives a message. A message has two parts to its header — a type and an address. The address specifies the relative position of the destination of the message. In a simple two-dimensional array the address might be of the form 'two up and six across'. Although this could be read as specifying a path, the actual path taken by a message depends on local conditions and is determined by the individual cells on the route. The action taken by the cell is determined by the rule table which is accessed by combining the local state (represented by the state vector) and the type of the message. Some registers contain relative addresses of other cells. Others are used for temporary storage of addresses and results of calculations.

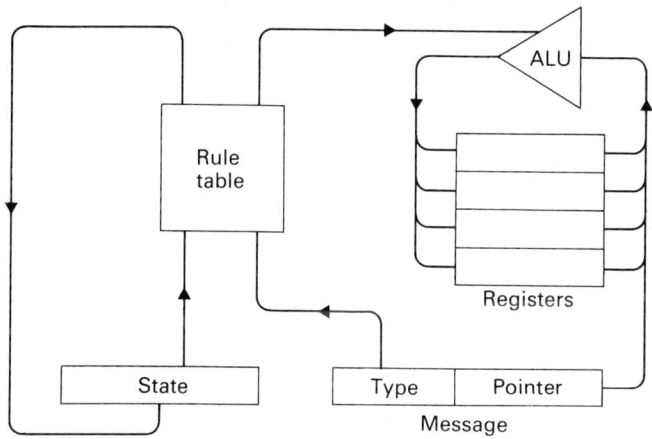

Fig. 14.1 Basic cell structure.

The network

Since the designers of the connection machine are talking about a network of millions of nodes, the design of a suitable communication network is clearly critical. The bandwidth of the network needs to be maximized within the constraints imposed by the need to provide physical connections. The highly connected hypercube network used by the designers of the CalTech Cosmic Cube becomes impractical with this number of nodes. The other extreme is the simple two-dimensional grid. This is easy to wire up, but internode distances become very large.

In the design for the connection machine, a family of connection strategies has been proposed. Consider the simple one-dimensional case shown in Fig. 14.2a. Here we have a single connection path joining adjacent nodes. If the nodes are arranged in a line then we get the connection pattern in Fig 14.2b. To increase the connectivity we can postulate that in addition to being connected to two adjacent nodes, each node is connected to the node farthest away (see Fig. 14.2c). This wiring pattern can be made efficient by forming a twisted and folded torus (Fig. 14.2d) where each node is adjacent to the node half way around the torus from it. This pattern can again be projected on to a line (Fig. 14.2e). To generate a two- or three-dimensional layout this process is repeated in each dimension.

Each connect, twist and fold operation halves the maximum connection distance, but doubles the wire density. The procedure may be repeated as many times as is desired in order to achieve an optimal trade-off between

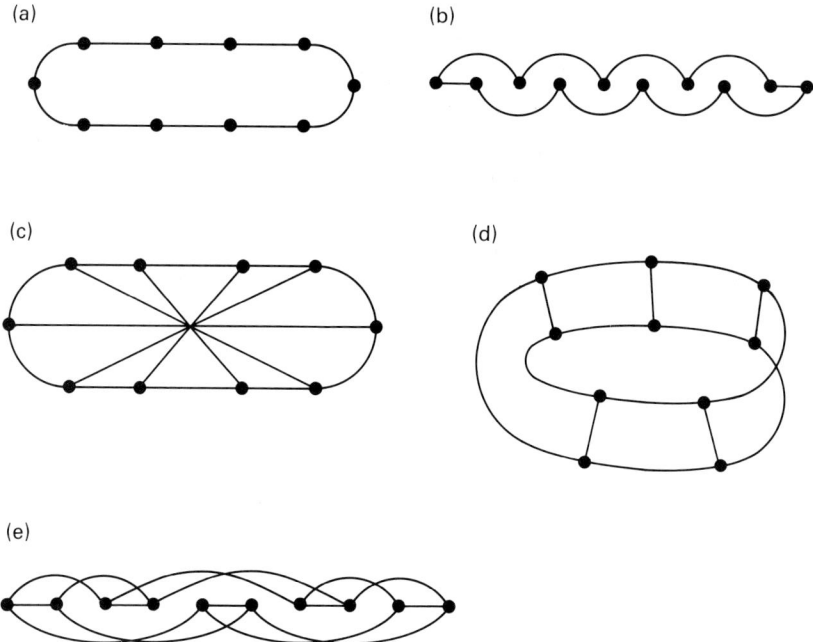

Fig. 14.2 Connection strategies.

performance and wireability. If the torus is twisted log(n) times where n is the number of nodes then the resulting structure is an augmented Boolean n-cube. As well as varying the number of connections, the width of the data connections can be varied. The original design for the connection machine recommended a two-dimensional connection pattern for use on a printed circuit board using a twice-folded torus with 5-bit data paths.

Using the connection machine

As with such designs as array processors, it is suggested initially that the connection machine be used in conjunction with a host processor which will see the connection machine as just another area of memory with rather unusual properties. The rule tables of all nodes are loaded from the host machine. Computation then proceeds in parallel. The possible operations can be grouped into four different types.

(1) Set operations. Some of the registers in the cells are called set registers which hold sets of nodes in the network. Register to register operations are therefore set operations.

(2) Propagation operations. Links between cells (logical not physical links) may be regarded as relations. As an example, consider a network of colours and objects. Links between objects and colours represent the relation 'has the colour'. To find the colour of an object we therefore have to apply 'the colour of' relation to a set containing that object. Now we imagine that some objects do not have a specific colour, but rather inherit it — for example if we define apples to be red then we can imagine crab-apples to be linked to apples by a relation 'kind of'. Crab-apples need not have a specific 'the colour of' link. It would be assumed that crab-apples inherited the redness property. The following operations would find all red objects

  a ← apply-reverse-relation (the colour of, {red})
  　　The set a contains all explicitly red things
  b ← complement({red})
  　　b is the set of all other colours
  b ← apply-reverse relation (the colour of, b)
  　　b is now the set of all explicitly non-red things
  b ← complement(b)
  　　b is all things not explicitly non-red
  c ← apply-reverse-relation (kind of, a, b)
  　　c is now all red things.

(3) Function manipulating operations. As well as apply function operations which are analogous to the apply relation operations discussed above, functions which manipulate the network are allowed. Consider the following sequence of operations to add a grandfather relation to a network which only records parents and sex

  a ← apply-reverse-relation (sex of, {male})
     a is the set of all males
  e ← identity function ( )
  f ← restrict (e, a)
     f is the identity function for males only.
     the function e has been restricted to apply
     only to members of a
  f ← compose (parent of, f, 1)
     f is now the father function
  g ← compose (parent of, f, 1)
     g is the one grandfather function using 1st parent
  insert(g, grandfather of)
     we add it to the network
  g ← compose (parent of, f, 2)
     g is the other grandfather function using 2nd parent
  insert(g, grandfather of)
     add this to the network .

(4) Arithmetic operations. Numbers are just regarded as special nodes and thus the arithmetic operations can be used in the same way as function operations.

Summary and further reading

We have outlined briefly a design proposal for a machine to implement large networks consisting of millions of nodes. Each node represents a data item and is associated with a simple processor cell. Although primarily designed for artificial intelligence, semantic networks and similar applications, other problems can be programmed in those terms. The connection pattern suggested could be adapted for general purpose multiprocessors or array processors. Once again we have another totally different approach to computing. Data and processing are closely linked and so we have truly decentralized computation. For further details of the design and the sorts of operation available the reader is referred to the paper by Hillis in *Physica* (Hillis, 1984). The Thinking Machine Corporation of Cambridge, Massachusetts is developing the connection machine and hope to have it available commercially soon.

This part has dealt with a number of different approaches to developing the future generations of computers. For those interested in the Japanese Fifth Generation Project a paper was published recently (Murakami *et al.* 1985).

Chapter 15

Summary and Conclusions

In this book we have attempted to provide an overview of distributed computing, parallel processing and the relationship between them. We saw that if we chose to we could view many existing computer systems as parallel and/or distributed processing systems. An attempt was made, however, to draw a distinction between systems which could be regarded as distributed or parallel and those which really were — and were therefore the subject of this book.

Many of the advantages claimed for distributed and parallel processing have already been claimed by many other developments, but we saw that there was some reason for believing that with distributed and parallel processing we might actually achieve some of them. Initially, the concept of parallelism was introduced and the ways in which computers have been developed to exploit the potential of parallel processing were discussed. We examined very briefly the nature of a simple parallel processing system consisting of two processors. We saw that increasing dependency decreases concurrency and noted that we had to be careful in our choice of timing values to avoid producing an artificial impression of the degree of parallelism. The same argument applied to our choice of task definition and to what we decided to include in our definition of a system.

The aim of parallel processing systems may be regarded as trying to increase the available computing power and the throughput as much as possible whilst keeping the cost increase to a minimum. Keeping the cost down usually involves the sharing of resources and/or increasing the interaction between the processors. In general, increased sharing of resources reduces the capital cost of a system, increases the contention and reduces the throughput. The possibility of contention is also increased by introducing interaction into a parallel processing system, and any method of resolving the contention leads to the possibility of one of the processors being idle for some time; thus reducing the potential increase in throughput and efficiency of adding a processor.

We summarized very briefly some of the major developments in parallel computer design, showing how the three initial approaches of array processors, pipelining and replication of functional units are all approaching the limits of their evolution. Most major work is now being

Summary and Conclusions 167

done on multiprocessors. Two designs were considered in more detail. These were the ICL Distributed Array Processor and the CalTech Cosmic Cube. We also looked at the transputer which has been proposed as a building block for future multiprocessors.

In Part 2 we turned to the topic of distributed processing. In this part we discussed the nature of distributed processing systems and showed how they are a logical concept which may or may not be mapped on to a physically distributed computer system. We considered the various levels at which distribution can occur and indicated briefly some of the interconnection structures which can be used. We also illustrated briefly by means of a simple example some of the factors which need to be considered in the design of a distributed computing system.

Part 3 was devoted to the programming of distributed and parallel systems. We looked at ways of finding the parallelism which exists in conventional programs as well as the ways of developing extra language features to express parallelism implicitly and explicitly. In particular, we looked at the ways in which programs can be developed for an array processor. The ways in which distributed processes could be synchronized when memory was shared were also discussed. The use of a Communicating Sequential Processes model was discussed with particular reference to the language occam developed by Inmos for use with its transputers.

In Part 4 we looked at some possible architectures which may form the basis of the next generation of computers. Ways in which the traditional structure of the von Neumann machine can be replaced by alternatives which more closely reflect new models of computation are discussed. These new models can help us to utilize fully the potential for parallelism which exists in many problems.

We introduced briefly the data flow approach as an alternative to the conventional von Neumann type model of computing and outlined some possible approaches to implementing this approach directly in hardware. The functional approach was introduced as a theoretical model for the data flow approach. This was rather misleading as the functional approach may be seen as the original approach to computation used by mathematicians before computers were invented. The reason for the renewed interest in what was once considered a purely academic approach is that we are now able to see possible ways of implementing this approach efficiently. We introduced briefly two possible machine architectures which seem to be heading towards the ultimate in decentralized control of computation.

Finally, we outlined briefly a design proposal for a machine to implement large networks consisting of millions of nodes. Each node represented a data item and was associated with a simple processor cell. Although primarily designed for artificial intelligence, semantic networks and similar applications, other problems can be programmed in those terms. The connection pattern suggested could be adapted for general purpose multiprocessors or array processors.

These final three approaches which attempt to utilize the intimate relationship between data and program are perhaps the most attractive line of research for future generations of computers

Further reading

Because of the introductory nature of this text, many of the topics referred to above were discussed without going into a great deal of detail. The aim of the various chapters can be seen as two-fold. Firstly, to introduce the reader to the general terminology used in a particular aspect of the subject and secondly, to motivate him or her to look in rather more detail into the topics discussed by following up some of the suggestions made for further reading. Obviously different readers will have found different chapters more interesting and it is unlikely that anyone will have either the time of inclination to follow up all the references given.

Despite the attempt to cover a fairly broad area and introduce most aspects of computer science which have been considered to be either distributed and/or parallel processing, there remains one important aspect of the subject which I have not mentioned. That is the formal treatment of distributed and parallel computing models. The nearest we have come to this field was in the brief introduction to Hoare's Communicating Sequential Processes model and in the chapters on Data Flow and Functional Programming. The only excuse I offer for the omission is that much of the formal treatment requires a lot of background terminology and mathematics to be covered before any useful work can be done. I feel, therefore, that it would be impossible to do justice to this aspect of distributed and parallel processing in an introductory text such as this. For the reader who feels a need to remedy this lack I would suggest that a reasonable starting point might be Section 5 of Chambers *et al.* (1984). Chapter 7 of Duce (1984) is also worth reading.

Cumulative Bibliography

Arvind & Kathail, V. (1981) A multiple processor data flow machine that supports generalized procedures. 8th Annual Symposium on Computer Architecture. *Computer Architecture News*, **9**,(3), 291–302.

Backus, J. (1978) Can programming be liberated from the von Neumann style? A functional style and its algebra of programs. 1977 ACM Turing Award Lecture. *Comm of the ACM*, **21**, (8), 613–41.

Baer, J. L. (1984) Computer architecture. *IEEE Computer*, **17**, (10), 77–87.

Ben-Ari, M. (1982) *Principles of Concurrent Programming*. Prentice-Hall, London.

Chambers, B. F., Duce, D. A. & Jones, G. P. (Eds) (1984) *Distributed Computing*. Academic Press, London.

Dennis, J. B. (1980) Data flow supercomputers. *IEEE Computer*, **13**, (11), 48–56.

Darlington, J. & Reeve, M. (1981) ALICE: a multiprocessor reduction machine for parallel evaluation of applicative languages. *ACM Conference on Functional Programming Languages and Computer Architectures*, 65–75.

Duce, D. A. (Ed) (1984) *Distributed Computing Systems Programme*. Peter Peregrinus Ltd for the IEE, London.

Evans, D. J. (Ed) (1982) *Parallel Processing Systems*. Cambridge University Press, Cambridge.

Feilmeier, M. (Ed) (1977) *Parallel Computers — Parallel Mathematics*. Proceedings of IMACS(AICA)-G1 Symposium, Munich, North-Holland, Amsterdam.

Feilmeier, M., Joubert, G. & Schendel, U. (Eds) (1983) *Parallel Computing 83*. Proceedings of International Conference on Parallel Computers, North-Holland, Amsterdam, 1984.

Flynn, M. J. (1966) Very high speed computing systems. *Proceedings of the IEEE*, **54**, (12), 1901–9.

Glaser, H., Hankin, C. & Till, D. (1984) *Principles of Functional Programming*. Prentice-Hall, London.

Gurd, J. R., Kirkham, C. C. & Watson, I. (1985) The Manchester prototype dataflow computer. *Comm of the ACM*, **28**, (1), 34–52.

Halsall, F. (1985) *Introduction to Data Communications and Computer Networks*. Addison-Wesley, London.

Hillis, W. D. (1984) The connection machine: a computer architecture based on cellular automata. *Physica*, **10D**, 213–28.

Hoare, C. A. R. (1978) Communicating sequential processes. *Comm of the ACM*, **21**, (8), 666–77.

Hoare, C. A. R. (1985) *Communicating Sequential Processes*. Prentice-Hall, London.

Hockney, R. W. & Jesshope, C. R. (1981) *Parallel Computers*. Adam Hilger Ltd, Bristol.

Holt, R. C. (1983) *Concurrent Euclid, The Unix System and Tunis*. Addison-Wesley, London.

Holt, R. C., Graham, G. S., Lazowska, E. D. & Scott, M. A. (1978) *Structured Concurrent Programming with Operating Systems Applications*. Addison-Wesley, London.

IEEE (1982) Data Flow Systems. *Computer* (Special Issue), **15**, (2).

IEEE (1982) Multiprocessing Technology. *Computer* (Special Issue), **18**, (6).

Inmos Ltd (1984) *Occam Programming Manual*. Prentice-Hall, London.

Jesty, P. H. (1985) *Networking with Microcomputers*. Blackwell Scientific Publications, Oxford.

Bibliography

Jones, G. (1987) *Programming in occam*. Prentice-Hall, London.
Keller, R. M., Lindstrom, G. & Patil, S. (1979) A loosely coupled applicative multiprocessing system. *AFIPS Conference*, **48**, 613–22.
Lorin, H. (1972) *Parallelism in Hardware and Software: Real and Apparent Concurrency*. Prentice-Hall, London.
Lorin, H. (1980) *Aspects of Distributed Computer Systems*. Wiley-Interscience, New York.
Mago, G. A. (1980) A cellular computer architecture for functional programming. *Digest of Papers, IEEE Computer Society COMPCON*, 179–87.
Murakami, K., Kakuta, T., Onai, R. & Ito, N. (1985) Research on parallel machine architecture for fifth generation computer system. *IEEE Computer*, **18**, (6), 76–92.
Paddon, D. J. (Ed) (1984) *Supercomputers and Parallel Computation*. Proceedings of Meeting at Bristol, September 1982, Oxford Clarendon Press, Oxford.
Rodriguez, G. (Ed) (1982) *Parallel Computations*. Academic Press, London.
Seitz, C. L. (1985) The Cosmic Cube. *Comm of the ACM*, **28**, (1), 22–33.
Sharp, J. A. (1985) *Data Flow Computing*. Ellis Horwood, Chichester.
Shore, J. E. (1973) Second thoughts on parallel processing. *Computers and Electrical Engineering*, **1**, (1), 95–109.
Stallings, W. (1984) *Local Networks — An Introduction*. Macmillan, New York.
Treleaven, P. C., Brownbridge, D. R. & Hopkins, R. P. (1982) Data-driven and demand-driven computer architecture. *ACM Computing Surveys* **14**, (1), 93–143.
Tiberghien, J. (Ed) (1984) *New Computer Architectures*. Academic Press, London.
Vegdahl, S. R. (1984) A survey of proposed architectures for the execution of functional languages. *IEEE Transactions on Computers*, **33**, (12), 1050–71.
Weitzman, C. (1980) *Distributed Micro/Minicomputer Systems*. Prentice-Hall, London.
Whitby-Strevens, C. (1985) The Transputer. 12th International Symposium on Computer Architecture, Boston. *Computer Architecture News*, **13**, (3), 292–300.

Index

abstract processor 1
acyclic loop 94
Alice design 156, 158
ACE 25
anti-dependency 101, 104
application partitioning 80
architectural speed-up techniques 23
   basic characteristics of 27
   relationships between 26
arithmetic level concurrency 32
array processors 24–25, 27, 34, 36, 39–46
   programming for 106–112
assignment statement 92
associative processors 28, 36
asymmetric system 13
asynchronous transmission 68
augmented boolean n-cube 163

Backus' FP 152–3
bit level concurrency 32
bit-parallel 28, 34
bit-serial 28, 34
block/wake-up synchronization 119, 121
boolean n-cube 163
boolean recurrence 104
Burroughs BSP 104
Burroughs D-825 28
Burroughs PEPE 28
busy waiting 118, 119

CalTech cosmic cube 46–49, 51, 147, 162, 167
Carnegie-Mellon C.mmp and C.m* projects 28
Carrier-Sense-Multiple-Access with Collision Detection (CSMA/CD) 74
CDC 6600 26, 28
CDC 7600 28
CDC CYBER 27, 29, 104
cedar project 29
circuit switching 69–73
classification schemes 33–37
   merits of 36
co-operative computing 77, 79
   typical system 21
cobegin/end construct 113–4
collision 75

Communicating Sequential Processes (CSP) 124–137, 142, 167
compound interconnection 65
concurrency 2, 12, 32
connection machine 159
   cells in 161
   network in 161
   operations in 163–4
connectivity 45, 110
constant generator 145, 151
contention 16, 22
control dependency 101, 103
control token 75
copy operation 151
coupled multicomputer systems 38
coupling 24, 37
   loose 57
   tight 57
CRAY-1 27, 104
Cray X-MP 28
critical regions 121
critical section 115, 117–8
CYBA-M 29
cyclic connectivity 110
cyclic dependencies 102–3

data flow computation 144
data flow computing 141
   functional approach 150, 167
data flow nodes 145
   firing rules for 143
data flow programs 141
   dynamic architecture for 146
   reconfigurable static architecture for 146
   static architecture for 145
data flow processor, generalized block diagram 147
data flow tokens 143
datagram approach 73
decomposed functional hierarchy 67
definition by cases 150
degrees of centralization 55
degrees of distributiveness 3
Dekker's algorithm 117
demand-driven evaluation 152
Denecolor HEP 29
dependency in programs 100–104
DEUCE 25

171

Index

disjoint processes 114
distributed processing 3
  potential for 6
  programming for 89
  reasons for 4
distributed system 2, 53
  candidates for 58–61
  design of 78–88
  fully 55–62
  heterogeneous example of 88
  typical organization with regional centre 59
  users view of 57–8
distribution
  levels of 63–4
  possible degrees of 65
dynamic architecture for data flow 146
dynamic self-scheduling 16

EDSACE 25
EDVAC 25
efficiency 16, 108
enqueue/dequeue 121
ETA/GF-10 29

fifth generation computers 139
firing rules (for data flow) 143
floating point operations per second (flops) 23
flow dependency 100, 141
Flynn's classification 33
  merits of 36–7
fork construct 113, 141
frame 75
fully distributed processing system 55–62
  definition of 56
functional approach 150–9
  partitioning 83–4
functional forms (in FP) 152–3
future computer architectures 139

gateway processor 83–4, 86
geographic partitioning 81–2
  at a central site 83
Goodyear Aerospace STARAN 28
graceful degradation 4
graph abstraction, principles of 104
graph reduction 156
guarded commands 128

hierarchic interconnection 65–6
hierarchical system, decomposed by application 68

horizontal partitioning 84–5
  replication for reliability 86
hypercube 29, 147, 161

IBM 308X 28
IBM 360 121
IBM 370 46, 121
IBM 701 26
IBM 7030 27
IBM 704 26
IBM 709 26
IBM 7090 26
IBM STRETCH 27
ICL Distributed Array Processor (DAP) 28, 41–5, 106–11
  FORTRAN for 109–11, 112
ILLIAC IV 28, 39–41
independent processes 114
INMOS transputer. *See* transputer
INTEL 80867 47
input dependency 101
instruction level concurrency 32
interaction 16
  effects of increasing 19
interconnection structures 63–70

jamming sequence 75
job level concurrency 32
join construct 113, 141

Lawrence Livermore S-1 project 29
lazy evaluation 152
levels of parallelism 32–3
linear recurrence 95, 98
Local Area Networks (LANs) 67, 74–6
logic-in-memory array 36
loop-free program segments 92
loops 93
  acyclic 94
  linear cyclic 95–6
  non-linear cyclic 98
loose coupling 37, 57

Mago's machine 154–5
Management Information System (MIS) 86, 88
Manchester data flow machine 147–8
memory interlock 116
message switching 69, 72–3
Mflop rate 46
monitor node 76
multifunction processors 24, 26, 33
multiple connection path systems 65, 70

Index

Multiple Execution Array processor (MEA) 37, 92
Multiple Execution Scalar processor (MES) 37, 92, 95–6, 98
Multiple Instruction stream Multiple Data stream processor (MIMD) 33–4, 36–7
Multiple Instruction stream Single Data stream processor (MISD) 33–4, 36–7
multiprocessors 23–4, 28–9, 34, 60
   definition of 39
   developing algorithms for 122
   an example 46
   possible shared memory architecture 60
mutexbegin/end construct 115–8
mutually exclusive access 115

networks 63–77
non-determinism 129
non-linear recurrence 98
nor operator 150

occam 51, 124, 142
   ALT construct 129
   FOR construct 132
   IF construct 129
   PAR construct 126
   SEQ construct 126
   WHILE construct 128
Orthogonal Mini EmbedmeNt (OMEN) 28
orthogonal processors 28
output dependency 101, 104

packet switching 69, 73–4
parallel
   architectures 32–52
   systems 2
parallel processing 3
   potential for 6
   programming for 89
   reasons for 4
parallelism 2
   and interaction 11–22
   brief history of 23–31
parbegin/end construct 113
partitioned distributed system 80–8
partitioning 80–7
   by application 80
   by responsibility 80
   functional 83–4
   geographical 81
   horizontal 84
   vertical 84
peer interconnection 65–6
   examples of 71

peripheral stand-alone computer system 37
permission token 75
pipelining 25, 27, 34, 36, 98
plane connectivity 110
process 1
processing, definition of 1
processor connectivity 45
program level concurrency 32
programming, with shared memory 113–23
programs, dependencies in 100–4
Propal-2 44–45

race condition 115
recurrence
   boolean 104
   linear 96
reconfigurable static architecture for data flow 146
reducible application 155
reduction 154–8
reliability 4, 85
   replication for 87
   replication of horizontal partitions for 86
replication of functional units. *See* multifunction processors
resource sharing 4, 21–2

scalar data 37, 91
self-scheduling 16
semaphores 118–21
shared memory, programming for 113–23
Shore's classification 34–6
   merits of 36–7
Simultaneous Operation Linked Ordinal Modular Network (SOLOMON) 27
simultaneous processing 2
Single Execution Array processor (SEA) 36, 92, 98
Single Execution Scalar processor (SES) 37, 92, 95
Single Instruction stream Multiple Data stream processor (SIMD) 33–4, 36–7
Single Instruction stream Single Data stream processor (SISD) 33–4, 36–7
single connection path systems 65, 69
slotted ring 76
speed-up 108
   architectural techniques for 23–5
statements, basic dependencies between 100–1
static architecture for data flow 145
string reduction 154
sub-tasks 11–2
symmetric independent multicomputer system 16

symmetrical system   13
synchronization   20, 24, 86, 112, 119, 121–2, 124
synchronous transmission   68

tasks   1, 11–2
  dependencies between   11
tight coupling   37, 57
time critical processes   115
tokens, data flow   143
transputer   29, 50
  block diagram of   50
  occam for   124
tree-height reduction   93, 104

UNIVAC 1   25
UNIVAC 1100/80   28
Utah lisp machine   148

vector data   91
vertical partitioning   84
virtual circuit approach   74
virtual machine   1

wavefront algorithm   96–7
  on n processors   99
Wide Area Networks (WANs)   67, 72